T0310650

Mastering Android Studio

Mastering Computer Science
Series Editor: Sufyan bin Uzayr

Mastering Android Studio: A Beginner's Guide
Divya Sachdeva and Reza Nafim

Mastering Swift: A Beginner's Guide
Mathew Rooney and Madina Karybzhanova

Mastering C++: A Beginner's Guide
Divya Sachdeva and Natalya Ustukpayeva

Mastering Git: A Beginner's Guide
Sumanna Kaul, Shahryar Raz, and Divya Sachdeva

Mastering Ruby on Rails: A Beginner's Guide
Mathew Rooney and Madina Karybzhanova

Mastering Sketch: A Beginner's Guide
Mathew Rooney and Md Javed Khan

For more information about this series, please visit: https://www.routledge.com/Mastering-Computer-Science/book-series/MCS

The "Mastering Computer Science" series of books are authored by the Zeba Academy team members, led by Sufyan bin Uzayr.

Zeba Academy is an EdTech venture that develops courses and content for learners primarily in STEM fields, and offers education consulting to Universities and Institutions worldwide. For more info, please visit https://zeba.academy

Mastering Android Studio

A Beginner's Guide

Edited by Sufyan bin Uzayr

CRC Press
Taylor & Francis Group
Boca Raton London New York

CRC Press is an imprint of the
Taylor & Francis Group, an **informa** business

First edition published 2022
by CRC Press

6000 Broken Sound Parkway NW, Suite 300, Boca Raton, FL 33487-2742

and by CRC Press
2 Park Square, Milton Park, Abingdon, Oxon, OX14 4RN

CRC Press is an imprint of Taylor & Francis Group, LLC

© 2022 Sufyan bin Uzayr

ISBN: 978-1-032-13412-3 (hbk)
ISBN: 978-1-032-13411-6 (pbk)
ISBN: 978-1-003-22907-0 (ebk)

DOI: 10.1201/9781003229070

Typeset in Minion
by KnowledgeWorks Global Ltd.

Contents

About the Editor

Sufyan bin Uzayr is a writer, coder, and entrepreneur with more than a decade of experience in the industry. He has authored several books in the past, pertaining to a diverse range of topics, ranging from History to Computers/IT.

Sufyan is the Director of Parakozm, a multinational IT company specializing in EdTech solutions. He also runs Zeba Academy, an online learning and teaching vertical with a focus on STEM fields.

Sufyan specializes in a wide variety of technologies, such as JavaScript, Dart, WordPress, Drupal, Linux, and Python. He holds multiple degrees, including ones in management, IT, literature, and political science.

Sufyan is a digital nomad, dividing his time between four countries. He has lived and taught in universities and educational institutions around the globe. Sufyan takes a keen interest in technology, politics, literature, history, and sports, and in his spare time, he enjoys teaching coding and English to young students.

Learn more at sufyanism.com.

CHAPTER 1

Introduction to Android Studio

IN THIS CHAPTER

➤ Getting to know the history of the Android platform

➤ Learning about Android Studio major benefits

➤ Reviewing Android Studio main features and characteristics

As a modern user, your choice of products can mean the difference between struggling and prospering. It is normal always to be searching for tools that increase productivity and optimize work. Specific tools have advantages that are so obvious that one adopts them immediately. Android Studio is one of them. The world was introduced to Android Studio just a few days after its prerelease at

Google's processing system in 2013. Before that premiered, we had been using Android Developer Tools (ADT) both professionally and as a learning tool. ADT is an Android development environment built upon the open-source integrated development environment (IDE) called Eclipse.

Android Studio is a product of a great collaboration between JetBrains and Google. Android Studio was built over JetBrain's IntelliJ, meaning that its functionality is a superset of IntelliJ. Almost anything you can do with IntelliJ, you should be able to do in Android Studio. Android Studio is revolutionary in the field because it streamlines the Android development process and makes Android development far more approachable than it has previously been.

Android Studio is now the official IDE for Android. The Android platform lets developers script managed code applying Java to operate and control the Android device. At the same time, Android Studio has replaced Eclipse as the IDE of choice for developing Android applications. Previously, the Android development was spread using the Eclipse platform with the Android Development Kit (ADK), provided by Google, which launched the Android Studio platform. The Android Studio IDE has some great advantages, for instance, the Gradle dependency manager, also based on IntelliJ, which is widely used all over the world. This application is one of the great strengths of the platform editor as it offers more options to the developer at build time.

Android Studio can be installed on Windows, OSX, and Linux operating systems. In addition, it is recommended by Google itself that the hardware must have at least 4 GB of memory and 1 GB of free hard disk space because, otherwise, Android Studio might be a little slow. You should also have Java installed on the machine via the Java Development Kit (JDK) since to develop on Android, and it is necessary for all Java development classes to be present on the machine.

Prior to its release, Android development was managed predominantly through Eclipse IDE, which offered a more generic Java IDE that with numerous other programming languages.

Now, it is safe to claim that Android Studio can make anyone's life significantly easier compared with nonspecialist software, but at the same time it still has a long way to go before it can certainly state to be a completely intuitive and smooth experience. For complete beginners, there is a lot to learn here, and much of the information available—even through official channels—can seem too dense to absorb at first.

This chapter will explain in a little more detail what Android Studio does and go over the basic functionality that you need to get started. We aim to keep everything as easy as possible, and hopefully, this will serve as the first step on your journey to Android development.

WHAT IS ANDROID STUDIO

Those of you without any prior experience in coding may be wondering about what exactly the Android Studio's role is when it comes to the development and what an IDE has to do with that anyway?

To start with, the Android Studio's responsibility is to provide the interface for you to create your applications and to operate much of the complex file management behind the scenes. The programming language you will be expected to use is either Java or Kotlin. If you opt for Java, this should be installed separately on your machine. Android Studio is simply a canvas where you will write, edit, and save your projects and the files that make up those projects. At the same time, Android Studio will give you access to the Android Software Development Kit (SDK). This should be viewed as an extension to the Java code that allows it to run smoothly on Android devices and take advantage of the native hardware. To put it simply, Java is necessary to script the programs, the Android SDK is needed to make those programs run on Android, and Android Studio has the job of assembling it all together for you. On the other hand, Android Studio also enables you to run your code through an emulator so that you will be able to "debug" the program as it operates and get feedback explaining crashes so that you can solve that problem faster.

Google has accomplished a great deal making Android Studio as powerful and useful as possible. For instance, they have added live hints so that while you are coding, you will get suggestions to make necessary changes that can fix errors or make your code sharper. Moreover, in case a variable is not being used, it will be highlighted in grey. And once you start typing a line of code, Android Studio will provide a list of autocomplete suggestions to help you finish it, which is great for when you cannot quite remember the correct syntax or you just want to save some time.

The following is a list of Android Studio's major releases:[1]

Version-Release date	
4.2	May 2021
4.1	October 2020
4.0	May 2020
3.6	February 2020
3.5	August 2019
3.4	April 2019
3.3	January 2019
3.2	September 2018
3.1	March 2018
3.0	October 2017
2.3	March 2017
2.2	September 2016
2.1	April 2016
2.0	April 2016
1.5	November 2015
1.4	September 2015
1.3	July 2015
1.2	April 2015
1.1	February 2015
1.0	December 2014

[1] https://developer.android.com/studio/releases, Android

TABLE 1.1   Basic System Requirements

	Microsoft Windows	**Mac**	**Linux**
Operating system version	Microsoft Windows 7/8/10 (32- or 64-bit) *The Android Emulator only supports 64-bit Windows.*	Mac OS X 10.10 (Yosemite) or higher, up to 10.14 (macOS Mojave)	GNOME or KDE desktop *Tested on gLinux based on Debian (4.19.67-2rodete2).*
Random-access memory (RAM)	4 GB RAM minimum; 8 GB RAM recommended.		
Free digital storage	2 GB of available digital storage minimum, 4 GB recommended (500 MB for IDE + 1.5 GB for Android SDK and emulator system image).		
Minimum required JDK version	Java Development Kit 8		
Minimum screen resolution	1280 × 800		

In addition, prior to installing the tool, it is recommended to see if you comply with the following basic system requirements shown in Table 1.1.[2]

Android Studio contains great tools such as the Android Virtual Device Manager and the Android Device Monitor. It also has Gradle toolkit that lets you automate and manage the build process, allowing you to determine flexible

---

[2] https://developer.android.com/studio, Android

custom build configurations. Other key features of Android Studio include the following:

- Support for a fast emulator
- Support for plenty of code templates and GitHub integration
- Support for template-based wizards for creating Android designs and components
- Support for rich layout editor
- Support for deep code analysis
- Support for an extensive set of tools and frameworks

On top of that, there are certain IntelliJ's code editor features that can enhance your productivity when building Android apps, such as:

- A unified environment where you can develop for all Android devices
- Apply changes to push code and resource changes to your running app without restarting your app
- Lint tools to catch performance, usability, version compatibility, and other problems
- C++ and Native Development Kit (NDK) support
- Built-in support for Google Cloud Platform, making it easy to integrate Google Cloud Messaging and App Engine

MAJOR FEATURES

Every project started in Android Studio contains one or more modules with source code files and resource files. Standard types of modules include Android app modules, Library modules, and Google App Engine modules.

Normally, Android Studio displays project files in the Android project view to provide quick access to your project's key source files. Thus, all the build files should be visible at the top level under Gradle Scripts, and each app module should have the following folders:

- *Manifests* holds the AndroidManifest.xml file.

- *Java* holds the Java source code files, including JUnit test code.

- *Res* holds all non-code resources, such as XML layouts, UI strings, and bitmap images.

The Android project architecture on disk is different from the typical flattened representation. It is also possible to customize the view of the project files to focus on specific aspects of your app development. For instance, selecting the Problems view of your project displays links to the source files holding any recognized coding and syntax errors, such as a missing XML element closing tag in a layout file.

The User Interface

The Android Studio main window consists of several main logical areas:

- The toolbar allows you to carry out a wide range of activities, such as running your app and launching Android tools.

- The navigation bar helps you to revise the project and select certain files for editing. It gives a more compact view of the overall structure visible in the project window.

- The editor window is where you script and edit code. Depending on the current file type, the editor can be modified. For example, when viewing a layout file, the editor shows the Layout Editor.

- The tool window bar runs around the outside of the IDE window and contains the buttons that let you expand or shrink individual tool windows.

- The tool windows give you access to specific tasks like project management, search, and version control. You can also expand or shrink them.

- The status bar is used to review the status of your project as well as the IDE, including all the warnings and messages.

Keep in mind that you can organize the main window to give yourself more screen space by hiding or moving toolbars and tool windows. You can also insert keyboard shortcuts to access most IDE functions.

Also, at any time, you can activate the search option across your source code, databases, actions, and elements of the user interface, just by double-pressing the Shift key or clicking the magnifying glass icon in the upper right-hand corner of the Android Studio window. This can be very helpful if you are trying to locate a particular IDE feature that you have forgotten how to activate.

Tool Windows

Instead of using preset options, Android Studio follows the original context to be able to automatically bring up relevant tool windows as you work. By default, the most commonly sought tool windows are pinned to the tool window bar at the edges of the application window.

- To expand or collapse a tool window, click the tool's name in the tool window bar. Here, you can also choose to drag, pin, unpin, attach, or detach tool windows.

- To return to the current default tool window layout, click Window > Restore Default Layout or customize your default layout by clicking Window > Store Current Layout as Default.

- To show or hide the entire tool window bar, click the window icon in the bottom left-hand corner of the Android Studio window.

- To locate a specific tool window, go over the window icon and select the tool window from the menu.

Or as an alternative, you can also use keyboard shortcuts to open tool windows:[3]

Tool window	Windows and Linux	Mac
1. Project	Alt+1	Command+1
2. Version Control	Alt+9	Command+9
3. Run	Shift+F10	Control+R
4. Debug	Shift+F9	Control+D
5. Logcat	Alt+6	Command+6
6. Return to Editor	Esc	Esc
7. Hide All Tool Windows	Control+Shift+F12	Command+Shift+F12

In case you need to hide all toolbars, tool windows, and editor tabs, click View > Enter Distraction Free Mode. This will enable Distraction Free Mode. And in order to exit

---

[3] https://developer.android.com/studio/intro, Android

Distraction Free Mode, click View > Exit Distraction Free Mode.

You can also activate Speed Search to search and filter within most tool windows in Android Studio. To use Speed Search, select the tool window and then type your search query.

In addition, Android Studio also has three types of code completion, which you can access using the following keyboard shortcuts given in Table 1.2.[4]

It is also possible to complete quick fixes and show intention actions by pressing Alt+Enter. Additionally, the Code Sample Browser in Android Studio can help you look for high-quality, Google-provided Android code samples based on the currently highlighted symbol in your project.

Navigation

We shall cover the navigation option in depth later in Chapter 4 of this book. But the basic features include the following:

You can *switch between your recently accessed files* applying the Recent Files action. To bring up the Recent Files action press Control+E (Command+E on a Mac) and by default, the last accessed file will be selected. You can also access any tool window through the left column in this action.

In case you need to *view the structure of the current file*, you can use the File Structure action. Bring up the File Structure action by pressing Control+F12 (Command+F12 on a Mac) and quickly navigate to any part of your current file.

---

[4] https://developer.android.com/studio/intro, Android

TABLE 1.2 Basic Keyboard Shortcuts

Type	Description	Windows and Linux	Mac
Basic completion	Displays basic suggestions for variables, types, methods, expressions, etc. If you call basic completion twice in a row, you see more results, including private members and non-imported static members.	Control+Space	Control+Space
Smart completion	Displays relevant options based on the context. Smart completion is aware of the expected type and data flows. If you call smart completion twice in a row, you see more results, including chains.	Control+Shift+Space	Control+Shift+Space
Statement completion	Completes the current statement for you, adding missing parentheses, brackets, braces, and formatting.	Control+Shift+Enter	Shift+Command+Enter

It is also possible to *search for and navigate to a specific class* in your project using the Navigate to Class action. Bring up the function by pressing Control+N (Command+O on a Mac) and go to Class supports sophisticated expressions, including camel humps, paths, line navigation, and middle name matching. If you call it twice in a row, it will display the results out of the project classes.

In order to *navigate to a file or folder* use the Navigate to File action. To bring up the Navigate to File action just press Control+Shift+N (Command+Shift+O on a Mac). To look for folders and not files, add a/at the end of your expression.

Navigate to a method or field by name using the Navigate to Symbol action. You can activate the Navigate to Symbol option by pressing Control+Shift+Alt+N (Command+Option+O on a Mac). Moreover, in order to find all the pieces of code referencing the class, method, field, parameter, or statement, you can press Alt+F7 (Option+F7 on a Mac).

Style and Formatting

Android Studio automatically applies formatting and styles as indicated in your code style settings as you go on to the editing process. You can customize the code style settings by programming language, including identifying conventions for tabs and indents, spaces, wrapping and braces, and blank lines. To customize your code style settings, follow the path: File > Settings > Editor > Code Style (Android Studio > Preferences > Editor > Code Style on a Mac.)

And even if the IDE automatically applies formatting as you script, you can also willingly call the Reformat Code action by pressing Control+Alt+L (Opt+Command+L on a Mac) or auto-indent all lines by pressing Control+Alt+I (Control+Option+I on a Mac).

Version Control Basics

As previously stated, Android Studio supports a variety of version control systems (VCS's), including Git, GitHub, CVS, Mercurial, Subversion, and Google Cloud Source Repositories.

After importing your app into Android Studio, you can access the Android Studio VCS menu options to enable VCS support for the needed VCS, create a repository, import the new files into version control, and complete other version control operations. In order to do that, from the Android Studio VCS menu, click Enable Version Control Integration. From the drop-down menu, select a VCS to link to the project root and then click OK. The VCS menu will then display a number of version control options based on the system you selected. It is also possible to activate the VCS via the File > Settings > Version Control menu option to set up and modify the version control settings.

Gradle Build System

Android Studio utilizes Gradle as the foundation of the build system, with more Android-specific capacities provided by the Android plugin for Gradle. This build system operates as an integrated tool from the Android Studio menu and independently from the command line. You can use the features of the build system to complete the following:

- Customize, configure, and extend the build process

- Create multiple Android application packages for your app, with different features using the same project and modules

- Reapply code and resources across various source sets

By employing the flexibility of Gradle, you can complete all of these without having to change your app's core source features. Normally, Android Studio build files are named build.gradle. They are treated as plain text files that use Groovy syntax to edit the elements provided by the Android plugin for Gradle. Each project has to have one top-level build file for the entire project and separate module-level build files for each module. Once you import an existing project, Android Studio automatically produces the necessary build files.

Build Variants

The build system assists in the creation of different versions of the same application from a single project. This is particularly useful when you have both a free version and a paid version of your app or in case you need to distribute multiple Android application packages for different device configurations on Google Play.

Multiple Android Application Package Support

Multiple Android application package support lets you create multiple packages based on screen density or application binary interface. For instance, you can create separate package support of an app for the hdpi and mdpi screen densities while still considering them a single variant and allowing them to share javac, dx, and ProGuard settings.

Resource Shrinking

Resource shrinking in Android Studio automatically gets rid of unused resources from your packaged app and library dependencies. For example, if your application is using Google Play services to access Google Drive functionality, and you are not currently using Google Sign In, then resource shrinking can delete the various assets for the Sign In buttons.

Managing Dependencies

Dependencies for your project are identified by name in the build.Gradle file. Gradle is responsible for searching for your dependencies and making them available in your build. You can declare module dependencies, remote binary dependencies, and local binary dependencies in your build.Gradle file. Android Studio configures projects to use the Maven Central Repository that is included in the top-level build file for the project by default.

Debug and Profile Tools

Android Studio also helps you in debugging and improving the performance of your code, including in-line debugging and performance analysis tools. You should apply in-line debugging to enhance your code walk-throughs in the debugger view with in-line verification of references, expressions, and variable values. In-line debug data function typically includes:

- In-line variable values
- Referring objects that reference a selected object
- Method's return values
- Lambda and operator expressions
- Tooltip values

In order to enable in-line debugging, go to the Debug window, click Settings and select the checkbox for Show Values In-line.

Performance Profilers

Android Studio provides performance profilers so you can track your app's memory and central processing unit usage, search deallocated objects, locate memory leaks, optimize graphics performance, and analyze network requests.

Heap Dump

When you are profiling memory usage in Android Studio, you can simultaneously initiate garbage collection and dump the Java heap to a heap snapshot in an Android-specific A Heap/CPU Profiling Tool (HPROF) binary format file. The HPROF viewer shows classes, instances of each class, and a reference tree to assist you in tracking memory usage and find memory leaks.

Memory Profiler

You can use Memory Profiler to trace memory allocation and check where objects are being placed when you perform certain actions. Being aware of these allocations enables you to optimize your app's capacity and memory use by analyzing the method calls related to those actions.

Data File Access

The Android SDK tools, such as Systrace and logcat, review performance and debug data for detailed app analysis. To see all the generated data files, open the Captures tool window. In the list of the generated files, double-click a file to view the data. After that, right-click at any .hprof files to convert them to the standard RAM usage file format.

Code Inspections

Every time you compile your program, Android Studio automatically runs configured Lint and other IDE inspections to help you identify and fix problems with the structural quality of your code.

The Lint tool revises your Android project source files for potential bugs and optimization improvements for correctness, security, quality, usability, accessibility, and internationalization. In addition to Lint checks, Android Studio also completes IntelliJ code inspections and verifies annotations to add to your coding workflow.

Annotations in Android Studio

Android Studio supports annotations for variables, parameters, and return values to help you prevent bugs, null pointer exceptions, and resource-type conflicts. The Android SDK Manager packages and the Support-Annotations library in the Android Support Repository could be used to validate the configured annotations during code inspection as well.

Log Messages

Once you build and run your app with Android Studio, you can view adb output and device log messages in the Logcat window. In case you need to profile your app's central processing unit, memory, and network performance, just access the Android Profiler by clicking View > Tool Windows > Android Profiler.

Sign in to Your Developer Account

You can sign in to your developer account in Android Studio to examine additional tools that require authentication, such as Cloud Tools for Android Studio and the App Actions test tool. By signing in, you give these tools authorization to administer and operate your data across Google services.

After you open a project in Android Studio, you can sign in to your developer account or switch developer accounts just by clicking the profile icon at the end of the toolbar to sign in. In the window that appears, you are expected to do one of the following: If you are not yet signed in, click Sign In and allow Android Studio to access the listed services. Or if you are already signed in, click Add Account to sign in with another Google account. Alternatively, you can click Sign Out and repeat the previous procedure to sign in to a different account.

A BRIEF HISTORY OF ANDROID STUDIO

The success story of Android goes back to 2003 when Andy Rubin, Rich Miner, Nick Sears, and Chris White cofounded a start-up called Android Inc. in Palo Alto, California. Later, the company was faced with the insufficiency of investment which brought Google into the picture. Google knew the product's true potential and sealed a deal worth $50 Million to acquire Android in 2005. That is how all four cofounders ended up at the Googleplex and continued to develop the OS further under their new owners. The first public Android Beta Version 1.0 was soon published on November 5, 2007.

Android is an outstanding computing platform based on the Linux operating system. The initial commercial version of Android took over the market in 2008 in the form of a mobile phone platform, back when the most popular cell phone for a business user was the BlackBerry, when the iPhone was just about to make meaningful steps across all sectors, and when the majority of phone users were still typing out texts from a flip phone.

Since that time, Android has certainly become one of the world's most popular operating systems by many measures. Despite the robust popularity of the modern and fashionable Apple iPhone platform, Android shipments worldwide meaningfully outpace Apple's offerings. And while Apple's devices continue to demand an ever-increasing price point, Android products scale the global marketplace. Surely, there are superexpensive Android models placed next to the latest iPhone, but there are also relatively low-cost Android phones and tablets available for sale at mass-market retailers.

Moreover, as Android has matured, it is finding its way into a variety of devices, including televisions, projectors, and automobiles. The latest include an Android-based touchscreen interface to manipulate the house controls and recreational vehicle's Android-based control system. To be clear, there are plenty of these types of interfaces finding their way to the market. This section aims to introduce the Android platform and discuss how you can use it for both mobile and nonmobile applications. The aim here is to prepare you on a path to making awesome apps for any platform you feel would be best to make your contribution.

The Android operating system is the largest installed base among different mobile platforms around the world. Hundreds of millions of mobile devices are powered by Android in more than 190 countries of the world. It conquered around 75% of the global market share by 2020,[5] and this trend is growing bigger every other day. Before Google acquired the whole company, the company consortium named Open Handset Alliance developed Android based on the modified version of the Linux kernel and

---

[5] https://gs.statcounter.com/os-market-share/mobile/worldwide, Statcounter

other open-source software. And in September 2008, the first Android-powered device was launched in the market. Android truly dominates the mobile OS industry because of the long list of features it serves. It is user-friendly, has great community support, and offers a greater extent of customization. As a result, we can observe a sharp increase in the market demand for developing Android mobile applications, and with that, companies search for smart developers with the right skill set. Initially, the purpose of Android was thought of as a mobile operating system. However, with the advancement of code libraries and its popularity among developers of different domains, Android becomes an absolute set of software for all devices like tablets, wearables, set-top boxes, smart TVs, and notebooks.

Android is a powerful open-source operating system that provides useful features that include the following:

- Android Open Source Project tool to customize the OS-based requirements.

- Android supports different types of connectivity for GSM, CDMA, Wi-Fi, and Bluetooth for telephonic conversation or data transfer.

- It contains multiple APIs to support location-tracking services such as GPS.

- We can manage all data storage-related activities by using the file manager.

- It contains a wide range of media supports like AVI, MKV, FLV, MPEG4, etc., to play or record a variety of audio/video.

- It also supports different image formats like JPEG, PNG, GIF, BMP, MP3, etc.

- It supports multimedia hardware control to perform playback or recording using a camera and microphone.

- Android has an integrated open-source WebKit layout-based web browser to support User Interfaces like HTML5, CSS3, etc.

- Android supports multitasking means that we can run multiple applications at a time and can switch in between them.

- It provides support for virtual reality or 2D/3D Graphics.

Google launched the first version of the Android platform on November 5, 2007. Since then, it has released a lot of other Android versions such as Apple Pie, Banana Bread, Cupcake, Donut, Éclair, Froyo, Gingerbread, Jellybeans, Kitkat, Lollipop, marshmallow, Nougat, and Oreo with extra functionalities and new features. The following list demonstrates the version details of android which is released by Google from 2007 to date.

Apple Pie	Android 1.0	September 23, 2008
Banana Bread	Android 1.1	February 9, 2009
Cupcake	Android 1.5	April 30, 2009
Donut	Android 1.6	September 15, 2009
Eclair	Android 2.0–2.1	October 26, 2009
Froyo	Android 2.2–2.2.3	May 20, 2010
Gingerbread	Android 2.3–2.3.4	December 6, 2010
Honeycomb	Android 3.0.x–3.2.x	February 22, 2011
Ice Cream Sandwich	Android 4.0–4.0.4	October 18, 2011

Jelly Bean	Android 4.1–4.1.2	July 9, 2012
KitKat	Android 4.4–4.4.4	July 9, 2012
Lollipop	Android 5.0–5.1	October 17, 2014
Marshmallow	Android 6.0–6.0.1	October 5, 2015
Nougat	Android 7.0–7.1	August 22, 2016
Oreo	Android 8.0	August 21, 2017
Pie	Android 9.0	August 6, 2018
Android Q	Android 10.0	September 3, 2019
Android 11	Android 11.0	September 8, 2020

Programming languages used in developing Android applications are Java and Kotlin. Previously, Java was considered the official language for Android development. But since 2017 Kotlin (developed and maintained by JetBrains) was used for developing the Android Application, as it was made an official language for Android Development.

ADVANTAGES OF ANDROID DEVELOPMENT

Since Android is an open-source operating system, it has a vast community for support. The design of the Android application has guidelines from Google, which becomes easier for developers to create more intuitive user applications. Fragmentation gives more potential to Android applications to be able to run multiple activities on a single screen. In addition, releasing the Android application in the Google play store is easier when it is compared to other platforms.

DISADVANTAGES OF ANDROID DEVELOPMENT

Although fragmentation provides a very intuitive approach for user experience, it still has some serious drawbacks, where the development team typically spends some time adjusting the various screen sizes of mobile smartphones that are now available in the market and activating particular features in the application.

At the same time, Android devices might vary broadly; therefore, the application testing becomes even more difficult. And as the development and testing take more time and other resources, the cost of the application might increase, depending on the application's complexity.

Since its introduction, Android is offered in the market by many players across the globe and across various industries. For example, Samsung might have evolved into the leading manufacturer of smartphone devices worldwide because of Android, and although a single device started it all, Android devices are now available in virtually every market on the planet—and not just for mobile phones.

It is beyond the scope of this chapter, but try asking yourself if there is no correlation between the world's most successful Internet/search company also being the driving force behind the world's most popular mobile platform. Thus, if you want to write code that can run and fly literally anywhere in the world, then you have picked the right time to learn about Android.

Looking at Android's breadth of capacities, it might be easy to confuse it with a desktop operating system. One has to perceive Android as a layered environment that is built upon a foundation of the Linux kernel and includes rich functionality across many areas. The user interface subsystem has everything one would expect from an evolved operating system environment, including windows, views, and widgets for displaying basic items like edit boxes, lists, or drop-down lists. The browser is both available for general web browsing and capable of embedding directly into your own application.

In the past decade, the mobile web has been greatly reshaped by the adoption of smartphones across consumer and business applications, including Android. Android has been able to embrace such responsive web technologies due to the major enhancement of the following software layers:

- Applications: built-in applications, such as phone, contacts, browser, and more. The adoption of several specific applications varies by Android version and manufacturer. Commercial applications from marketplaces, such as Google Play, Amazon, and others.

- Enhancing application frameworks, such as cell manager, location manager, notification manager, content providers, windowing, and resource manager.

- Advancing capacity of libraries, such as graphics libraries, media libraries, database libraries, sensors, etc.

- The Android runtime is responsible for executing and managing applications as they run. Here, we should mention Linux Kernel, including power, file system, drivers, and process management.

In addition, Android has a vast array of connectivity options, including Wifi, Bluetooth, NFC, and cellular connections on every network that you can imagine. You can also access any location-based services that power popular mapping and navigation apps. Digital cameras have essentially retreated up-market due to the quality of the cameras installed in modern smartphones. Android supports multiple cameras with the ability to capture full-motion video.

One of the popular classes of applications is machine vision, where applications use the camera as an input device to perform inspections for manufacturing. The installation of voice-based services has also turned the modern Android device into a virtual personal assistant.

Clearly, if you can imagine it, you can program it on the Android platform. An important point of the Android application environment is that Android applications have historically been written in the Java programming language. We have already mentioned that Android is now running on a relatively new programming language called Kotlin. However, in case you are just starting out, Java is a safe place to explore for a couple of reasons. First, there is a decade's worth of Android resources on the web focused on Java. Second, Java is a language that still has potential in it for other platforms—particularly server-side web technologies. As a classic object-oriented programming language, Java skills still matter.

While it might not matter as much at this point, but there are some interesting details around how Android applications come to life from their underlying source code. Java source code is established and formatted into bytecode, which represents the logic of an application but not the specific requirements for a particular hardware device. Like traditional Java environments, early versions of Android operated by converting the so-called bytecodes to hardware-specific executable codes. This conversion procedure is normally achieved using a Just-In-Time (JIT) compiler and takes place each time the application is implemented. Once the JIT compiler has converted the code, it is executed in a virtual machine known as the Dalvik VM.

But beginning with Android version 4.4 (KitKat), the Dalvik VM has been removed. The JIT compiler converts bytecodes to executable code directly on the device at runtime, each time the application runs. This new approach is called Ahead-of-Time (AOT) compilation. With AOT compilation, the byte code is converted only once when the application is installed. This slows down the one-time activity of installing the application but gives the benefit of faster implementation at run time when it is really necessary.

Because of AOT, we can enjoy a faster runtime experience with lower RAM requirements at the expense of more storage requirements. Taking into consideration the slow decline in the cost of storage, this looks like an agreeable direction to move in for mobile applications.

At the same time, regardless of the moving pieces of how applications get converted from source code to running code, from a programming perspective, there are some basic principles to understand before starting out with Android development.

To start with, Android application consists of one or more of the following four classifications:[6]

- **Activities:** An application that has a visible user interface is implemented via an activity. Once you select an application from the home screen or application launcher, an activity is started.

- **Services:** You can use a service for any application that needs to persist for a long time, such as a network monitor or update-checking application.

---

[6] https://developer.ibm.com/technologies/mobile/articles/os-android-devel/, Developer

- **Content providers:** The easiest way to think about content providers is to see them as database servers. A content provider's responsibility is to manage access to persisted data, such as the contacts on a phone. If your application is very simple, you might not necessarily create a content provider, but if you are building a larger application or one which makes data available to multiple activities and/or applications, a content provider is the proscribed means of accessing your data.

- **Broadcast receivers:** You can launch an Android application to process a specific element of data or respond to an event, such as receiving a text message.

An Android application is deployed to a device in a package with a file named AndroidManifest.xml. This file is required for every Android application and is basically the regulation sheet that dictates the operating system exactly how to interact with your application. The AndroidManifest.xml includes both the required class names and types of events that the application is able to undertake as well as the required permissions that the application has to run. To illustrate with an example, if an application requires access to the network to download a file, this permission should be explicitly stated in the manifest file. Or, for instance, an application needs to access the camera. The user must approve that also. This approach of notably regulating the user about what the application is going to use is vital in this day of increasing privacy and security issues. While you can quickly just accept software licenses, it is essential to pay close attention to what an app is requesting to access.

EXPLORING ANDROID STUDIO

The easiest way to get started with developing Android applications is to explore the Android Studio application suite. You can download a copy of Android Studio for your preferred platform (Windows®, Mac OS X, or Linux) from the Android developer's site. Android Studio includes tools for managing multiple platform-specific features with the sdkmanager and the ability to test your application on either a real device or the emulator.

There are older generations of development tools, including ADT, which is the predecessor to Android Studio, and Eclipse with an ADT plug-in, which was the predecessor to ADT. To be precise, Android Studio is the third generation of the Android IDE. There are also command-line tools and various continuous integration toolchains that allow to build Android applications.

You might consider starting with Java code. Scripting in Java within Android Studio is intuitive because it provides a rich Java environment, including context-sensitive help and code suggestion notes. Once you compile your Java code cleanly, the components of Android Studio make sure all of the application is set properly, including the AndroidManifest.xml file.

Enough background at this point. Let's take a look at the installation process and development environment required to build an Android application.

CHAPTER 2

Getting Started with Android Studio

IN THIS CHAPTER

➤ Learning how to install and configure Android Studio

➤ Acquire competence in Gradle Build Scripts

➤ Review and start working with Android Studio projects

In the previous chapter, we learned about the history of the Android platform and its main characteristics and advantages. This chapter shall walk you through installing and setting up your development environment so you can follow the instructions and examples in this book. First, we shall look at the installation and configuration process, review Gradle Build Scripts and learn more about working with Android Studio projects.

INSTALLATION AND CONFIGURATION

Setting up Android Studio has to normally take just a few clicks. Yet first things first, make sure you download the latest version 4.2.2 (June 2021) of Android Studio from the official Developer's site: https://developer.android.com/studio.

Windows

If you are installing Android Studio on Windows, be sure to proceed with the following steps: In case you downloaded an .exe file, just double-click to launch it. If you downloaded a.zip file, you first need to unpack the ZIP, copy the android-studio folder into your Program Files folder, and then open the android-studio > bin folder and launch studio64.exc (for 64-bit machines) or studio.exe (for 32-bit machines).

You can later follow the setup wizard in Android Studio and install any other packages that it recommends. As new tools and products become available, Android Studio will let you know with a pop-up notification, or you can always check for updates by clicking Help > Check for Update.

Mac

If you are a Mac user, the setup process is pretty straight-forward as it is:

- First, launch the Android Studio DMG file.

- Then move and locate Android Studio into the Applications folder, after that launch Android Studio.

- Choose whether you want to import previous Android Studio settings or not and then click OK.

The Android Studio Setup Wizard will guide you through the rest of the setup, which includes downloading Android software development kit items that are crucial to ensure better performance. As new tools and products become available, Android Studio will let you know with a pop-up notification, or you can always check for updates by accessing Android Studio > Check for Updates.

Additionally, if you use Android Studio on MacOS Mojave, you will probably get a prompt to permit the integrated development environment (IDE) to look through your calendar, contacts, or photos. This prompt is introduced by a new privacy protection technique for applications that access files under the home directory. Thus, if your project has files and libraries in your home directory, and this prompt occurs, you can always go with the Do Not Allow option.

Linux

In order to install Android Studio on Linux, proceed as follows:

Unpack the .zip file you downloaded to a suitable location for your applications, such as within /usr/local/ for your user profile, or /opt/ to share with others. In case you are using a 64-bit version of Linux, you need to install the required libraries for 64-bit machines first. But at the same time, if you are running a 64-bit version of Ubuntu, you should install some 32-bit libraries with the following command:[1]

```
sudo apt-get install libc6:i386
libncurses5:i386 libstdc++6:i386 lib32z1
libbz2-1.0:i386
```

Or if you are operating 64-bit Fedora, the command is:

```
sudo yum install zlib.i686 ncurses-libs.
i686 bzip2-libs.i686
```

When launching Android Studio, open a terminal, proceed to the android-studio/bin/directory, and activate studio. sh. Select whether you need to import previous Android Studio settings or not, then press OK.

The Android Studio Setup Wizard guides you through the rest of the setup, which includes downloading Android

---

[1] https://developer.android.com/studio/install, Android

key components that are required for the development. In order to add Android Studio to your list of applications, go to Tools > Create Desktop Entry from the Android Studio menu bar.

As new tools and products become available, Android Studio will let you know with a pop-up notification, or you can always check for updates by accessing Help > Check for Update.

Chrome OS

If you are a Chrome OS user, follow these steps for full installation:

- In case you have not already done so, install Linux for Chrome OS.

- Open the Files app and locate the DEB (Debian Software Package file) you downloaded in the Downloads folder under My files.

- Right-click the DEB package and select Install with Linux (Beta).

- Choose the target file location for DEB package on Chrome OS.

- If you have installed Android Studio previously, select whether you want to import basic Android Studio settings again or not, then click OK.

The Android Studio Setup Wizard is there to take you through the rest of the setup, which also includes downloading Android key development components. And once the installation is complete, launch Android Studio either from the Launcher or from the Chrome OS Linux terminal by running the following studio.sh in the default installation directory:

```
/opt/android-studio/bin/studio.sh
```

Similarly, as new tools become available, Android Studio will let you know through a pop-up, or you can see those updates by clicking Help > Check for Update.

Moreover, Android Studio provides wizards and templates that explain your system requirements, such as the Java Development Kit (JDK), and configure default settings, such as an optimized default Android Virtual Device (AVD) emulation and updated system images. We are going to look through each of these documents and additional configuration settings later in Chapter 4 of this book. But just to go over some basic configuration procedures, Android Studio provides access to two configuration files through the Help menu:

- **studio.vmoptions:** Used to customize options for Studio's Java Virtual Machine (JVM), such as heap size and cache size. Typically, on Linux machines, this file is named studio64.vmoptions, depending on your version of Android Studio.

- **idea.properties:** Applied to customize Android Studio properties, such as the plugins folder path or maximum supported file size.

Both configuration files are located in the configuration folder for Android Studio. The name of the folder depends on your Studio version. Here are the locations for Android Studio 4.1 and higher:

- **Windows**
  Syntax: %APPDATA%\Google\<product><version>
  Example: C:\Users\YourUserName\AppData\Roaming\ Google\AndroidStudio4.1

- **MacOS**
  Syntax: ~/Library/Application Support/Google/<pro duct><version>
  Example: ~/Library/Application Support/Google/ AndroidStudio4.1

- **Linux**
  Syntax: ~/.config/Google/<product><version>
  Example: ~/.config/Google/AndroidStudio4.1

As Android Studio versions 4.0 and lower, configuration files are located in the following places:

- **Windows:** %USERPROFILE%\.CONFIGURATION_ FOLDER

- **MacOS:** ~/Library/Preferences/CONFIGURATION_ FOLDER

- **Linux:** ~/.CONFIGURATION_FOLDER

Another simple way to locate your configuration directory is to go to Help > Edit Custom VM Options in Android Studio. This option opens a configuration file and lets you inspect the path of the configuration file to see your con-figuration directory.

You can also use the following environment variables to reach particular override files elsewhere:

- **STUDIO_VM_OPTIONS:** Set the name and location of the .vmoptions file.

- **STUDIO_PROPERTIES:** Set the name and location of the .properties file.

- **STUDIO_JDK:** Set the JDK with which to run Studio.

Customizing Your VM Options

The studio.vmoptions configuration file lets you modify options for Android Studio's JVM. To enhance Studio's performance, the most common way is to adjust is the maximum heap size, but you can also use the studio.vmoptions file to change other default settings such as initial heap size, cache size, and Java garbage collection switches.

In order to create a new studio.vmoptions file or to open your existing one, click Help > Edit Custom VM Options. In case you have never edited VM options for Android Studio before, the IDE prompts you to open a new studio. vmoptions file. Click Yes to open the file.

The studio.vmoptions file then will be available in the editor window of Android Studio. Edit the file to add your own customized VM options. The studio.vmoptions file you make will then get added to the default studio.vmoptions file, located in the bin/directory inside your Android Studio installation folder.

However, it is not recommended that you directly edit the studio.vmoptions file found inside the Android Studio program folder. Even if you can access the file to view Studio's default VM options, editing only your own studio. vmoptions file ensures that you do not change key default settings for Android Studio. Thus, in your studio.vmoptions file, modify only the attributes you care about and permit Android Studio to continue using default values for any items you have not touched.

Now, by default, Android Studio's maximum heap size is 1280 MB. If you are working on a large project and your system has a lot of RAM, you can advance performance by increasing the maximum heap size for Android Studio processes, such as the core IDE, Gradle daemon, and Kotlin daemon. But at the same time, Android Studio will automatically check for possible heap size optimizations and notify you if it sees that performance can be improved.

If you use a 64-bit system that has at least 5 GB of RAM, you can also change the heap sizes for your project manually. To do so, just click File > Settings from the menu bar (or Android Studio > Preferences on MacOS). Then navigate to Appearance & Behavior > System Settings > Memory Settings. Here you can adjust the heap sizes to serve your desired amounts. When done, click Apply. At the same time, if you changed the heap size for the IDE, you should restart Android Studio before the new memory settings are saved. Also, keep in mind that allocating too much memory can very possibly degrade your overall performance.

When it comes to IDE settings, you can export a Settings.jar file that holds all or a segment of your preferred IDE settings for a project. You can then import the Java Archive (JAR) file into your other projects and make the JAR file accessible to your colleagues to incorporate into their projects.

Customizing Your IDE Properties

To customize IDE properties, apply the idea.properties file that will let you adjust IDE properties for Android Studio, such as the path to user-installed plugins and the maximum file size supported by the IDE. The idea.properties file then consolidates with the default properties for the IDE so you can pick just the override properties.

To make a new idea.properties file or to access your existing file, go through the following steps: Click Help > Edit Custom Properties. In case you have not edited the IDE properties before, Android Studio asks you to create a new idea.properties file. Simply click Yes to make the file. The idea.properties file will then become available in the editor window of Android Studio. Edit the file to add your own customized IDE properties.

Configuring the IDE for Low-Memory Machines

If you are running Android Studio on a machine with less than the recommended memory specifications, you can still customize the IDE to improve processes on your machine by taking the following actions:

- **Updating Gradle and the Android plugin for Gradle:** Update the latest versions of Gradle and the Android plugin for Gradle to make sure you are adopting the latest improvements for performance.

- **Enabling Power Save Mode:** Enabling Power Save Mode turns off a number of memory- and battery-intensive background operations, including error highlighting and on-the-fly inspections, autopopup code completion, and automatic incremental background compilation. To turn on Power Save Mode, click File > Power Save Mode.

- **Disabling unnecessary lint checks:** To change which lint checks Android Studio activates on your code, click File > Settings (on MacOS, Android Studio > Preferences) to open the Settings dialog. In the left pane, expand the Editor section and click Inspections. Click the checkboxes to select or deselect lint checks as appropriate for your project. Click Apply or OK to save your modifications.

- **Debugging on a physical device:** Debugging on an emulator takes more memory than debugging on a physical device, so you can enhance overall performance for Android Studio by debugging on a physical device.

- **Including only necessary Google Play services as dependencies:** Including Google Play Services as dependencies in your project increases the amount of memory necessary. Therefore, make sure to only include necessary dependencies to improve memory usage and performance.

- **Do not enable parallel compilation:** Android Studio typically compiles independent modules in parallel, but if you have a low-memory system you should not turn on this feature. To revise this setting, click File > Settings (on MacOS, Android Studio > Preferences) to open the Settings dialog. In the left pane, expand Build, Execution, Deployment, and then click Compiler. Here, make sure that the Compile independent modules in the parallel option are unchecked. Once you have made a modification, click Apply or OK for your change to take effect.

Setting the JDK Version

A copy of the latest OpenJDK is included in the Android Studio 2.2 and higher, and this is the JDK version we recommend you use for your Android projects. In order to activate and apply the bundled JDK, proceed with the following:

Open your project in Android Studio and go to File > Settings > Build, Execution, Deployment > Build Tools > Gradle (Android Studio > Preferences> Build, Execution, Deployment > Build Tools > Gradle on a Mac). Under Gradle JDK, opt for the Embedded JDK option and click OK.

By default, the Java language version used to script your project is based on the compileSdkVersion since different versions of Android support different versions of Java. Therefore, if needed, you can change this default Java version by adding the following CompileOptions {} block to your build.Gradle file:

```
android {
    compileOptions {
        sourceCompatibility JavaVersion.
VERSION\_1\_6
        targetCompatibility JavaVersion.
VERSION\_1\_6
    }
}
```

Proxy Settings

Proxies could be defined as intermediary link points between HTTP clients and web servers that are responsible for ensuring the security and privacy of internet connections. In order to support running Android Studio behind a firewall, it is necessary to set the proxy proper for the Android Studio IDE. You can use the Android Studio IDE HTTP Proxy settings page to set the HTTP proxy settings for Android Studio. From the menu bar, navigate to File > Settings (on MacOS, click Android Studio > Preferences). In the left pane, you should click on Appearance & Behavior > System Settings > HTTP Proxy. When the HTTP Proxy page appears, opt for Auto-detect proxy settings if you need to use an automatic proxy configuration URL for the proxy settings, or you can click on Manual proxy configuration to be able to enter each of the settings yourself. Click Apply or OK to save your changes.

Android Plugin for Gradle HTTP Proxy Settings

When running the Android plugin from the command line or on machines where Android Studio is not yet installed, access the Android plugin for Gradle proxy settings through the Gradle build file. If you need to access application-specific HTTP proxy settings, set the proxy settings in the build.Gradle file as required for each application module. As for project-wide HTTP proxy settings, set the proxy settings in the Gradle/Gradle.properties file.

One has to understand that Android Studio performance on Windows can be affected by a variety of circumstances or contributions. From now we shall see how you can optimize Android Studio settings to achieve the best possible conduction on Windows.

The easiest thing you can start from would be minimizing the influence of antivirus software on build speed. Generally, some antivirus software tends to interfere with the Android Studio build process, resulting builds to operate significantly slower. Once you start a build in Android Studio, Gradle compiles your app's resources and source code and then holds the compiled resources together in an APK. During this stage, multiple files are created on your computer. And if your antivirus software has a real-time scanning function turned on, the antivirus can push the build process to slow down each time a file is made while the antivirus tracks and scans that file.

To prevent this from happening, you should disable certain directories from real-time scanning in your antivirus software. However, to ensure that your computer is safe from malicious attacks, you must not completely disable real-time scanning or your antivirus software. The following is the list of the default location of each Android Studio directory that you need to be excluded from real-time scanning:

- **Gradle cache:** %USERPROFILE%\.gradle

  - **Android Studio projects:** %USERPROFILE%\ AndroidStudioProjects

  - **Android SDK:** %USERPROFILE%\AppData\ Local\Android\SDK

Android Studio system files:

- **Syntax:** %LOCALAPPDATA%\Google\<product> <version>

- **Example:** C:\Users\YourUserName\AppData\Local\ Google\AndroidStudio4.1

In case you face Group Policy limiting the number of directories you can exclude from real-time scanning on your computer, you can always move your Android Studio directories to one of the locations that the centralized Group Policy already cuts out.

Here we have illustrated how you can customize the location of each Android Studio directory, where C:\WorkFolder is the directory that your Group Policy already rejects:

- **For Gradle cache:** Define the GRADLE_USER_ HOME environment variable to refer to C:\ WorkFolder\.gradle.

- **For Android Studio projects:** Move or insert new project directories in an appropriate subdirectory of C:\WorkFolder. For example, C:\WorkFolder\AndroidStudioProjects.

- **Follow these instructions for Android SDK:** In Android Studio, open the Settings dialog (Preferences on MacOS), then move to Appearance & Behavior > System Settings > Android SDK. Change the value of Android SDK Location to C:\WorkFolder\AndroidSDK. To refrain from downloading the SDK again, you should just copy the existing SDK directory, located at %USERPROFILE%\AppData\Local\Android\SDK by default, to the new location.

- **For Android Studio system files:** Open Android Studio then proceed to Help > Edit Custom Properties. Android Studio will ask you to create an idea.properties file if you do not already have one. Here, make sure to insert the following line to your idea.properties file:

- idea.system.path=c:/workfolder/studio/caches/trunk-system

THE USE OF GRADLE BUILD SCRIPTS

Gradle is the name of an automated Android-based toolkit that permits the way in which projects are made to be modified and administered through a combination of various configuration files. This includes determining how a project is to be scripted, what dependencies have to be brought about for the project to build successfully, and what the end output of the build procedure should look like.

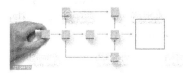

The main advantage of Gradle lies in the adaptability that it offers to the user. The Gradle system positions itself as a self-sufficient, command-line-based setting that can be incorporated into other project setting through the plug-in application. In the case of Android Studio, Gradle integration is performed through the similarly named Android Studio Plug-in application.

Although the Android Studio Plug-in ensures that Gradle tasks are initiated and managed from within Android Studio, the Gradle command-line wrapper can still be applied to start Android Studio-based projects on systems on which Android Studio is not installed. The configuration rules to commence a project are regulated by Gradle build files and scripts are based on the Groovy programming language.

Gradle brings a number of outstanding characteristics to building Android application projects. Some of the main features are discussed in the following sections.

Sensible Defaults

Gradle is founded on a concept referred to as convention over configuration. Simply put, it means that Gradle has a pre-determined number of sensible default configuration settings that will be applied by default unless they are disabled by settings in the build files. This also means that builds can be administered with the minimum configuration adjusted by the developer. Changes to the build files are only required when the default configuration does not fill all of your build specifications.

Dependencies

Another key item that ensures Gradle functionality is that of dependencies. For instance, a module within an Android Studio project activates a motion to load another module in the project. The first module has a dependency on the second module since the application will fail to build if the second module cannot be found and launched at runtime. This dependency can be observed in the Gradle build file for the first module so that the second module is attached in the application build, or a random error in the event of the second module cannot be found or built. Other examples of dependencies could be libraries and JAR files on which the project relies to compile and run.

Typically, Gradle dependencies are classified as local or remote. A local dependency stands for an item that is located on the local file system of the computer on which the build is being operated. A remote dependency, on the other hand, refers to an item that is located on a remote server (also named as a repository).

Most times remote dependencies are handled for Android Studio projects through another project management product named Maven. In case a remote dependency is established in a Gradle build file using Maven syntax, then the dependency will be downloaded automatically from the identified repository and added to the build process. The following dependency declaration, for example, causes the AppCompat library to be included in the project from the Google's repository: Implementation 'com.android.support:appcompat-v7:26.0.2'.

Build Variants

In addition to previously mentioned tools, Gradle also has a build variant support for Android Studio projects. This allows multiple variations of an application to be created from a single project. And since Android operates on many different devices encompassing a range of processor types and screen sizes it is important to target as many device types and sizes as possible to be able to build a number of different variants of an application (with a user interface for phones as well as for tablet-sized screens). Now, through the extensive use of Gradle, it is possible in Android Studio.

Manifest Entries

It is considered acceptable that every Android Studio project has accompanied with it an AndroidManifest.xml file holding configuration data about the application. A number of manifest entries can be defined in Gradle build files which are then auto-generated into the manifest file when the project is executed. This capacity is strictly additional to the build variants feature, allowing features such as the application version number, application ID, and SDK version information to be modified differently for each build version.

ProGuard Support

ProGuard is a tool that comes with Android Studio that optimizes, merges, and compiles Java byte code to make it more productive but at the same time more difficult to reverse engineer (the method by which the rationale of an application can be understood by others through analysis of the compiled Java byte code). The Gradle build files provide the ability to regulate whether or not ProGuard is activated on your application when it is built.

Gradle is an open-source system that is also used to automate project building, testing, and deployment. Build. gradle are scripts where you can optimize the tasks. Every Android project needs a gradle for generating an apk from the .java and .xml files in the project. Simply put, a gradle takes all the source files (java and XML), converts them into dex files and compresses all of them into a single file known as apk.

There are two types of build.gradle scripts: top-level build.gradle and module-level build.gradle. Top-level build.gradle is located in the root project directory, and its main goal is to determine which build configurations have to be applied to all the modules in the project.

The top-level build.gradle supports the following build configurations:[2]

- **Buildscript:** Used to configure the repositories and dependencies for Gradle.

- **Dependencies:** This block in buildscript is utilized to configure dependencies that the Gradle needs to build during the project.

- **All projects:** This is the block where one can modify the third-party plugins and libraries. For freshly

---

[2] https://developer.android.com/studio/build/gradle-tips#groovy, Android

created projects android studio includes JCenter and Google's maven repository by default.

- **Task clean(type:Delete):** Used to remove the directory every time the project is activated. This way the project keeps clean when someone edits some configuration files like settings.gradle which require a complete clean environment.

Module-level build.gradle is located in the project/module directory of the project. This particular grade script is where all the dependencies are defined and SDK versions are verified. The script has many functions in the project, which includes additional build types and settings modifications in the main app manifest or top-level build.gradle file.

The Module-level build.gradle supports the following build configurations:[3]

- **Android:** This block is used for configuring the specific android build options.
  compileSdkVersion – This is used to set the API level of the app so that the app can use the features of this and the lower level.

- **defaultConfig:** applicationId – This is used for identifying unique id for publishing of the app.
  minSdkVersion – This defines the minimum API level required to run the application.

---

[3] https://developer.android.com/studio/build/gradle-tips#groovy, Android

targetSdkVersion – This defines the API level used to test the app.

versionCode – This defines the version code of the app. Each time app will require an update, the version code has to be increased by 1 or more.

versionName – This defines the version name for the app.

- **buildTypes(release):** minifyEnabled – This is used to enable code shrinking for release build.

  proguardFiles – This is used to specify the project settings file.

  Dependencies – This is used to specify the dependencies that are required to build the project.

Both the top-level and module-level build.gradle files should be perceived as the main script files for automating tasks in android project and used by Gradle for generating the APK from the source files. And if you are new to Gradle, here are some configurations to manage your project's modules and their sources:

Changing Default Source Set Configurations

It is possible to use the sourceSets block in the module-level build.gradle file to change where Gradle refers to gather files for each component of a source set. For projects that administer multiple modules, it might be useful to define properties at the project level and allocate them across all modules. You can also do this by adding extra properties to the ext block in the top-level build.gradle file.

Managing Libraries and Dependencies
In addition, Gradle also has a robust mechanism to manage dependencies, whether they're remote libraries or local library modules. If you need to establish a dependency for only a specific build variant source set or testing source set, just make sure to capitalize the dependency configuration name and prefix that to the name of the build variant or testing source set.

Creating Different Versions of Your App
Gradle and the Android plugin let you create different versions of your app from a single module by configuring build variants. With the Android plugin, you can start multiple APKs that each target Application Binary Interface (ABI) or screen density and take advantage of Google Play's Multiple APK support.

But in case if you want to create separate APKs for different screen densities, add the android.splits.density block to your module's build.Gradle file. In order to create separate APKs for each ABI, you would have to add the android. splits.abi block to your module's build.Gradle file.

By default, when Gradle runs APKs for your project, each APK has the same version information as stated in the module-level build.gradle file. Because the Google Play Store does not permit multiple APKs for the same app that all have the same version information, you need to make sure that each APK has its own unique versionCode before you upload it to the Play Store. You can do this with custom build logic that distributes a different version code to each APK at build time.

Configuring Instrumentation Manifest Settings

When Gradle builds your test APK, it automatically sets up the AndroidManifest.xml file and configures it with the <instrumentation> node. It is possible to change some of the settings for this node by either generating another manifest file in the test source set or configuring your module-level build.gradle file.

Originally, all tests run against the debug build type. You can change this to another build type by adding the testBuildType property in your module-level build.gradle file. To illustrate, if you want to run your tests against your "production" build type, modify the file in the following snippet-fashion:

```
android {
    ...
    testBuildType "production"
}
```

Configuring Gradle Test Options

In case you want to specify which particular options change how Gradle runs all your tests, configure the testOptions block in the module-level build.gradle. In addition, you can also make use of the following configurations to help speed up your full and incremental builds.

Shrink Your Code: Android Studio uses R8 tool that converts our java byte code into an optimized dex code. It goes through the whole application and optimizes unused classes and methods. It runs on the compile-time and reduces the size of the build to make it more solid. For new projects, Android Studio uses a default settings file (proguard-android.txt) from the Android SDK's tools/ proguard/folder. Thus, if you need more code shrinking than R8 provides, try modifying the proguard-android-optimize.txt file:

```
android {
 buildTypes {
  release {
   minifyEnabled true
   proguardFiles getDefaultProguardFile
('proguard-android-optimize.txt'),
      'proguard-rules.pro'
   }
  }
  . . .
```

Sign Your App   Even though Android Studio provides a simple path to configure signing for release builds from the UI, as an alternative, you can also manually edit the signingConfigs block in your module's build.gradle file. All signing configurations are typically stored as plain text in the module's build.gradle file. So if you are working with a team or an open-source project, you can move what might be confidential information out of the build files by proceeding as follows:[4]

First, create a file named keystore.properties in the root directory of your project and include the following information:

storePassword=myStorePassword

keyPassword=myKeyPassword

---

[4] https://developer.android.com/studio/build/gradle-tips#groovy, Android

keyAlias=myKeyAlias

storeFile=myStoreFileLocation

Second, in your build.gradle file, you need to load the keystore.properties file in the following manner (this has to be before the android block):

//Creates a variable called keystorePropertiesFile, and initializes it to the

//keystore.properties file.

```
def keystorePropertiesFile = rootProject
.file("keystore.properties")
```

//Initializes a new Properties() object called keystoreProperties.

```
def keystoreProperties = new Properties()
```

//Loads the keystore.properties file into the keystoreProperties object.

```
keystoreProperties.load(new FileInputStream
(keystorePropertiesFile))
android {
    …
}
```

Once you are done with that, just input the signing information stored in the keystoreProperties object:

```
android {
  signingConfigs {
    config {
```

```
      keyAlias keystoreProperties
['keyAlias']
      keyPassword keystoreProperties
['keyPassword']
      storeFile file(keystoreProperties
['storeFile'])
      storePassword keystoreProperties
['storePassword']
    }
  }
  . . .
```

At last, make sure to click Sync Now in the notification bar.

Simplify App Development   In order to simplify app development, it is recommended to share custom fields and resource values with your app's code. Thus, during build time, Gradle generates the BuildConfig class so your app code can potentially inspect all the data about the current build. Here, you can also insert custom fields to the BuildConfig class from your Gradle build configuration file using the buildConfigField() method and access those values in your app's runtime code. Similarly, you can also include app resource values with resValue().

Share Properties with the Manifest   In several instances, you may need to declare the same property in both your manifest and your code (for example, when declaring authorities for a FileProvider). Instead of updating the same property in multiple locations to reflect a change, you can identify a single property in your module's build.gradle file to make it available to both the manifest and your code.

By default, each Android Studio project holds a Gradle wrapper tool for the purpose of authorizing Gradle tasks to be requested from the command line. This tool is located in the root directory of each project folder. Even though this wrapper is executable on Windows systems, it still needs to have the permission enabled on Linux and MacOS before it can be utilized. To enable such permission, you need to access a terminal window and change the directory to the project folder for which the wrapper is needed, and execute the following command:

```
chmod +x gradlew
```

When the file has executed permissions, the location of the file will either need to be included in your $PATH environment variable, or the name prefixed by ./ in order to run. For example: ./gradlew tasks.

Generally, Gradle treats project building in terms of a number of different tasks. A full listing of tasks that are available for the current project can be retrieved by activating the following command from within the project directory (make sure you prefix the command with a ./ if running on MacOS or Linux): gradlew tasks.

In order to build a debug release of the project suitable for device or emulator testing, appl the assembleDebug option: gradlew assembleDebug.

Alternatively, to build a release version of the application, you can insert: gradlew assembleRelease.

For the most part, Android Studio is fully able to manage application builds in the background without any intervention from the developer. This build process runs with the use of the Gradle system that is designed to review the ways in which projects are built to be configured through a set of build configuration files. And while the standard behavior of Gradle is sufficient for many basic project build requirements, the need to modify the build process is inevitable when it comes to more complicated projects.

WORKING WITH PROJECTS

A project in Android Studio holds everything that defines your workspace for an app; this includes source code, assets, test code, and build configurations. When you start a new project, Android Studio creates the necessary composition for all your files and makes them visible in the Project window (via View > Tool Windows > Project). This page normally contains a whole overview of the key components inside your project.

Modules

A module is one of the key items of the project. It stands for a collection of source files and build settings that let you divide your project into separate units of execution. Your project can have one or many modules and one module may use another module as a dependency. Nevertheless, you can be sure that each module can be independently built, tested, and debugged.

Additional modules are often used to create different code libraries within the project or if you need to have multiple sets of code and resources for different device types, such as phones and wearables, but at the same time ensure that all the files are scoped within the same project and share some code. You can add a new module to your project by clicking File > New > New Module.

Android Studio has a few other distinct types of modules:

Android App Module

Acts as a container for your app's source code, resource files, and app-level settings such as the module-level build file and Android Manifest file. When you create a new project, the default module name is "app." In the Create New Module window, Android Studio has the following types of app modules to choose from:

- Phone and Tablet Module
- Wear OS Module
- Android TV Module
- Glass Module

They each hold key files and code templates that are suitable for the corresponding app or device type.

Feature Module

This module type represents a modularized feature of your app that is closely related to Play Feature Delivery. For instance, with feature modules, you can provide your users with specific features on-demand or instant experiences through Google Play Instant.

Library Module

Provides a location for your reusable code, which you can apply as a dependency in other app modules or can use with other projects. Judging strictly by structure, a library module resembles app module a lot, yet when built, it results in a code archive file instead of an APK, so it cannot be installed on a device. In the Create New Module window, Android Studio presents the following library modules:

- **Android Library:** This type of library can hold all file types supported in an Android project, including source code, resources, and manifest files. The end result is an Android Archive (AAR) file that you can include as a dependency for your Android app modules.

- **Java Library:** This type of library can hold only Java source files. The build result is a JAR file that you can include as a dependency for your Android app modules or other Java projects.

Google Cloud Module

Google Cloud module is a perfect container for your Google Cloud backend code. This module has the required code and dependencies for a Java App Engine backend that uses simple HTTP, Cloud Endpoints, and Cloud Messaging to connect to your app. With that, you can develop your backend to provide cloud services for your app.

Applying Android Studio to develop and manage your Google Cloud module lets you regulate app code and backend code in the same project. You can also run and test your backend code locally, as well as deploy your Google Cloud module through Android Studio.

It is considered a norm to perceive modules as subprojects because Gradle refers to modules as projects. For example, when you create a library module and want to add it as a dependency to your Android app module, you should declare it as an implementation project like this:

```
dependencies {
    implementation project
    (':my-library-module')
}
```

Project Files

By default, Android Studio keeps your project files in the Android view. However, this view does not reflect the actual file structure on disk, but simply organized by modules and file types to let you navigate between key source files of your project, or be able to remove certain files or directories that are not often used. Some of the structural adjustments compared to the structure on disk include the following:

- You can look through all the project's build-related configuration files in a top-level Gradle Script group.

- You can see all manifest files for each module in a module-level group (when you have different manifest files for different products and build types).

- You can access all alternative resource files in a single group, instead of in separate folders per resource qualifier. For instance, all density versions of your launcher icon were made visible side-by-side.

In order to review the actual file structure of the project including all files hidden from the Android view, select Project from the dropdown at the top of the Project window. When you click Project you will be able to access the most important files and directories as follows:[5]

- **build/:** Contains build outputs.

- **libs/:** Contains private libraries.

- **src/:** Contains all code and resource files for the module.

- **androidTest/:** Contains code for instrumentation tests that run on an Android device.

- **main/:** Contains the "main" source set files: The Android code and resources shared by all build variants (files for other build variants reside in sibling directories, such as src/debug/ for the debug build type).

- **AndroidManifest.xml:** Describes the nature of the application and each of its components.

---

[5] https://www.programmersought.com/article/35024001299/, ProgrammerSought

- **java/:** Contains Java code sources.

- **jni/:** Contains native code using the Java Native Interface (JNI).

- **gen/:** Contains the Java files generated by Android Studio, such as your R.java file and interfaces created from Android Interface Definition Language (AIDL) files.

- **res/:** Contains application resources, such as drawable files, layout files, and UI strings.

- **assets/:** Contains file that should be compiled into an .apk file as-is. You can navigate this directory in the same way as a typical file system using uniform resource identifiers (URIs) and read files as a stream of bytes using the AssetManager. For example, this is a good location for textures and game data.

- **test/:** Contains code for local tests that run on your host JVM.

- **build.gradle (module):** This defines the module-specific build configurations.

- **build.gradle (project):** This defines your build configuration that applies to all modules. This file is integral to the project, so you should keep them in revision control with all other source code.

Project Structure Settings

In order to change various settings for your Android Studio project, open the Project Structure dialog by clicking File > Project Structure. It has the following main sections:

- **SDK Location:** Sets the location of the JDK, Android SDK, and Android NDK that your project uses.

- **Project:** Coordinates the version for Gradle and the Android plugin for Gradle, and the repository location name.

- **Modules:** Let you edit module-specific build configurations, including the target and minimum SDK, the app signature, and library dependencies. The Modules settings section allows you to change configuration options for each of your project's modules. Each module's settings page consists of the following tabs:

  - **Properties:** Specifies the versions of the SDK and build tools to utilize when compiling the module.

  - **Signing:** Identifies which certificate to use to sign your APK.

  - **Flavors:** This lets you create multiple build variants, where each flavor specifies a set of configuration settings, such as the module's minimum and target SDK version, and the version code and version name. For instance, you might define one flavor that has a minimum SDK of 15 and a target SDK of 21, and another flavor that has a minimum SDK of 19 and a target SDK of 23.

  - **Build Types:** This lets you create and modify build configurations. By default, every module has debug and release build types, but you can define more as needed.

- **Dependencies:** Lists the library, file, and module dependencies for this module. You can add, modify, and delete dependencies from this section.

Now, let's try and go through the creation of a new Android project with Android Studio. The procedure is pretty simple and requires you to go through the following simple steps.

Once you installed the latest version of Android Studio, in the Welcome to Android Studio window, click Create New Project. If you have a project already opened, select New Project. In the Select a Project Template window, select Empty Activity and click Next. In case you would like to place the project in a different folder, change its Save location. Select either Java or Kotlin from the Language drop-down menu and select the lowest version of Android you need your app to support in the Minimum SDK field.

You would also be able to access the Help me choose link in the Android Platform Distribution dialog. This dialog provides information about the different versions of Android that are distributed among devices. The key point to consider is the percentage of Android devices you need to support as well as the amount of work to maintain your app on each of the different versions that those devices operate on. For instance, if you opt for making your app compatible with many different versions of Android, you increase the effort that is required to maintain compatibility between the oldest and newest versions.

In case your app requires standard legacy library support, mark the Use legacy android.support libraries checkbox. Leave the other options unchanged as they are and click Finish. After some processing time, the Android Studio main window appears to give you a chance to take a moment to review the most important files.

Here, be sure the Project window is open and the Android view is selected from the drop-down list at the top of that window. At this point, you should be able to see the following files:

app > java > com.example.myfirstapp > MainActivity

This is the main activity file. It holds the entry point for your app. The system automatically launches an instance of this Activity and loads its layout when you build and run your app.

app > res > layout > activity_main.xml

This XML file defines the layout for the activity's user interface. It holds the standard TextView element with the text "Hello, World!"

app > manifests > AndroidManifest.xml

This manifest file determines the fundamental characteristics of the app and defines each of its items.

Gradle Scripts > build.gradle

There are two files with this name: One for the project, "Project: My_First_App," and one for the app module, "Module: My_First_App.app." Each module has its own build.gradle file, but fundamentally you can use each module's build.Gradle file to regulate how the Gradle plugin builds your app.

Choosing Your Project

In case you do not have a project opened yet, Android Studio displays the Welcome screen, where you can open a new project by clicking Start a new Android Studio project. You should then follow the Create New Project wizard, which lets you select the type of project you want to create and populates it with code and resources to get you started.

In the Choose your project screen that appears with the wizard, you can select the type of project you want to create from categories of device form factors, which are presented as tabs near the top of the wizard. In the first screen of the wizard, choose the type of project you want to create. By selecting the type of project you want to create, Android Studio can include sample code and resources to guide you further. After you make a decision, just click Next.

Configuring Your Project

The next step would be to configure some settings and creating your new project. Configuration of a new project takes just a few settings. Make sure you specify the Name of your project as well as the Package name. By default, this package name also becomes your application ID, which you can always change later.

You would also need to specify the Save location where you need to locally place your project. In addition, select the Language you want Android Studio to apply when creating sample code for your new project. But remember that you are not limited to using only that language creating the project. After that, select the Minimum API level you want your app to support. Once you select a lower API level, your app can rely on fewer modern Android APIs. However, a larger percentage of Android devices are able to run your app. The opposite is also true when selecting a higher API level.

In case you need your project to utilize AndroidX libraries by default, which stand for an improved version of the Android Support libraries, check the box next to the Use AndroidX item. When you are ready to create your project, simply click Finish.

Android Studio can create your new project with just basic code and minimum resources. However, if you later decide to add support for a different device form factor, you can include a module in your project later. And if you want to share code and resources between modules, you can do so by establishing an Android library.

Import an Existing Project

To import an existing, local project into Android Studio, proceed as follows: Go to File and click on Import Project. In the window that appears, navigate to the root directory of the project you want to import and click OK. Android Studio then starts the project in a new IDE window and indexes its contents. If you are importing a project from version control, use the Project option from the Version Control menu.

Feature Module Build Configuration

When you create a new feature module using Android Studio, the IDE applies the following Gradle plugin to the module's build.Gradle file: Apply plugin: 'com.android. dynamic-feature'.

The majority of the properties available to the standard application plugin are also available to your feature module. However, there are certain properties that are not recommended to include in your feature module's build configuration.

Since each feature module depends on the base module, it also inherits certain configurations. Thus, you should omit the following in the feature module's build.gradle file:

- **The minifyEnabled property:** You can activate code shrinking for your entire app project from only the base module's build configuration. Therefore, you might want to omit this property from feature modules. You can, however, add specific ProGuard rules for each feature module.

- **Signing configurations:** App bundles are signed using signing configurations that you specify in the base module at the start.

- **versionCode and versionName:** When building your app bundle, Gradle uses app version information that the base module provides. Therefore, there is no need to provide additional details using these properties.

Establish a Relationship to the Base Module

When Android Studio manages your feature module, it makes sure it is visible to the base module by adding the android.dynamicFeatures property to the base module's build.gradle file, as illustrated below:[6]

```
//In the base module's build.Gradle file.
android {
    ...
    //Specifies feature modules that have
a dependency on
    //this base module.
    dynamicFeatures = [":dynamic_feature",
":dynamic_feature2"]
}
```

Moreover, Android Studio also includes the base module as a dependency of the feature module in the following manner:

```
//In the feature module's build.Gradle
file:
...
dependencies {
    ...
    //Declares a dependency on the base
module, ':app'.
    implementation project(':app')
}
```

Specify Additional ProGuard Rules

Although only the base module's build configuration may authorize and regulate code shrinking for your app project,

---

[6] https://developer.android.com/guide/playcore/feature-delivery, Android

you can set custom ProGuard rules with each feature module using the proguardFiles property, as shown here:

```
android.buildTypes {
    release {
        // You must use the following
property to specify additional ProGuard
        // rules for feature modules.
        proguardFiles 'proguard-rules-
dynamic-features.pro'
    }
}
```

It is important to keep in mind that these ProGuard rules are merged with those from other modules (including the base module) at build time. Meaning that while each feature module may define a new set of rules, those rules apply to all modules in the app project.

Deploy Your App

While you are setting your app with various support for feature modules, it is also possible to deploy it to a connected device like you normally would by clicking the Run function from the menu bar. Yet in case your app project includes one or more feature modules, you can select which features to add when deploying your app by modifying your existing run/debug configuration as follows: Go to Run > Edit Configurations from the menu bar and review the Run/Debug Configurations dialog on the left panel to select your desired Android App configuration. Under Dynamic features to deploy in the General tab, go through the box next to each feature module you want to include when deploying your app. Once you made up your mind, just click OK.

At the same time, Android Studio does not typically deploy your app using app bundles to deploy your app. Instead, the IDE builds and installs APKs to your device that are optimized for deployment speed, rather than APK size.

Use Feature Modules for Custom Delivery

A great benefit of feature modules is the capacity to customize how and when different features of your app are downloaded onto devices running Android 5.0 (API level 21) or higher. For instance, to reduce the initial download size of your app, you can modify certain features to be either downloaded as needed on-demand or only by devices that support certain capabilities, such as the ability to take pictures or support augmented reality characteristics.

Even if you get highly optimized downloads by default when you upload your app as an app bundle, the more improved and suitable feature delivery options require more configuration and modularization of your app's features using feature modules. Meaning that feature modules stand as building blocks for creating modular features that you can later configure so each could be downloaded as needed.

Let's take an app that you want your users to buy and sell goods in an online marketplace from. With feature modules, you can effectively modularize each of the following functionalities of the app into separate feature modules:

- Account login and creation
- Browsing the marketplace

- Placing an item for sale

- Processing payments

Table 2.1 demonstrates the different delivery options that feature modules support and states how they might be used to optimize the initial download size of the sample marketplace app.[7]

Building a URI for a Resource

At times you might need to access a resource stored in a feature module. The easiest way to do that would be through a URI using Uri.Builder():[8]

```
val uri = Uri.Builder()
 .scheme(ContentResolver.
 SCHEME_ANDROID_RESOURCE)
 .authority(context.getPackageName()) //
 Look up the resources in the application
 with its splits loaded
 .appendPath(resources.
 getResourceTypeName(resId))
 .appendPath(String.format("%s:%s",
 resources.getResourcePackageName(resId),
 // Look up the dynamic resource in the
 split namespace.
 resources.getResourceEntryName(resId)
 ))
 .build()
```

---

[7] https://developer.android.com/guide/playcore/feature-delivery, Android
[8] https://developer.android.com/guide/playcore/feature-delivery, Android

TABLE 2.1 Features Delivery Options

Delivery Option	Behavior	Sample Use-Case	Getting Started
Install-time delivery	Feature modules that do not configure any of the delivery options are downloaded at app install, by default. This is an important behavior because it means that you can adopt advanced delivery options gradually. In addition, your app can request to uninstall features at a later time. So, if you require certain features at app install, but not after that, you can reduce install size by requesting to remove the feature from the device.	You can include that feature at app install, by default. However, to reduce the installed size of the app, the app can request to delete the feature after the user has completed the training.	Modularize your app using feature modules that configure no advanced delivery options.
On-demand delivery	Allows your app to request and download feature modules as needed.	You can configure the feature module to be downloaded only when a user shows interest in placing items for sale in the marketplace. Additionally, if the user no longer sells items after a certain period of time, the app can reduce its installed size by requesting to uninstall the feature.	Create a feature module and configure on-demand delivery. Your app can then use the Play Core library to request to download the module on demand.

(Continued)

TABLE 2.1 (Continued)   Features Delivery Options

Delivery Option	Behavior	Sample Use-Case	Getting Started
Conditional delivery	Allows you to specify certain user device requirements, such as hardware features, locale, and minimum API level to determine whether a modularized feature is downloaded at app install.	In order to reduce the initial app download size, you can create separate feature modules for processing certain types of payment methods and have them installed conditionally on a user's device based on their registered locale.	Create a feature module and configure conditional delivery.
Instant delivery	Google Play Instant allows users to interact with your app without needing to install APK(s) on their device. Instead, they can experience your app through the "Try Now" button on the Google Play Store or a URL that you create. This form of delivering content makes it easier for you to increase engagement with your app.	You can instant-enable that module so that users can instantly experience the game through a URL link or "Try Now" button, without app installation.	Create a feature module and configure instant delivery. Your app can then use the Play Core library to request to download the module on demand.

Each segment of this path to the resource is built at run time, ensuring that the correct namespace is created after the split APKs have been loaded. As an example of how the URI is generated, suppose you have an app and feature modules with these names:

- **App package name:** com.example.my_app_package

- **Feature's resources package name:** com.example. my_app_package.my_dynamic_feature

If the resId in the code snippet above refers to a raw file resource named "my_video" in your feature module, then the Uri.Builder() code above would result in the following: android.resource://com.example.my_app_package/ raw/com.example.my_app_package.my_dynamic_ feature:my_video

This URI can then be utilized by your app to access the feature module's resources. To verify the paths in your URI, you can use the APK Analyzer to track your feature module APK and determine the package name or use the APK Analyzer to inspect the package name in a compiled resource file.

Considerations for Feature Modules

Using feature modules, it is possible to considerably improve build speed and engineering velocity and extensively customize the delivery of your app's features to shrink your app's size. But at the same time, there are certain constraints and limitations to keep in mind when using feature modules:

- Installing 50 or more feature modules on a single device, through conditional or on-demand delivery, might result in serious operational failures. Install-time modules, which are not treated as removable, are automatically included in the base module and only count as one feature module on each device.

- Make sure to limit the number of modules you modify as removable for install-time delivery to ten. Otherwise, the download and install time of your app might surge.

- Keep in mind that only devices running Android 5.0 (API level 21) and higher support downloading and installing features on demand.

- Feature modules should not mark activities in their manifest with android:exported set to true. That is mainly because there could be no guarantee that the device has downloaded the feature module when another app tries to launch the activity. Meaning, your app should verify that a feature is downloaded before trying to access its code and resources.

- When introducing a new feature module using Android Studio, the IDE adds most of the manifest attributes that the module requires to behave like a feature module.

In addition, some attributes are included by the build system at compile-time, so there is no need for you to specify or edit them yourself. The following list outlines the manifest attributes that are important to feature modules:

1. **<manifest…:** This is the standard <manifest> block.

2. **xmlns:dist=http://schemas.android.com/apk/distribution:** Specifies a new dist: XML namespace.

3. **split="split_name":** Defines the name of the module, which your app specifies when requesting an on-demand module using the Play Core Library. When Android Studio builds your app bundle, it adds this attribute by default. Therefore, there is no need to include or modify this attribute yourself.

   To put it simply, when you create a feature module using Android Studio, the IDE uses what you specify as its Module name to identify the module as a Gradle subproject in your Gradle settings file. And when you build your app bundle, Gradle applies the last element of the subproject path to insert this manifest attribute in the module's manifest. To illustrate, if you create a new feature module in the MyAppProject/features/ directory and specified "basic_feature1" as its Module name, the IDE adds ':features:basic_feature1' as a subproject in your settings.Gradle file. When building your app bundle, Gradle then injects <manifest split="basic_feature1"> in the module's manifest.

4. **android:isFeatureSplit="true | false">:** Specifies that this module is a feature module. When Android Studio builds your app bundle, it attaches this attribute by default. Thus, you should not add or modify this attribute manually.

5. **<dist:module:** This new XML element defines attributes that determine how the module should be packaged and distributed as APKs.

6. **dist:instant="true | false":** Specifies whether the module should be available through Google Play Instant as an instant experience.

In case your app includes one or more instant-enabled feature modules, you must also instant-enable the base module. When using Android Studio 3.5 or higher, the IDE does this for you when you create an instant-enabled feature module. You cannot set this XML element to true while also setting <dist:on-demand/>. Nevertheless, you can still request on demand downloads of your instant-enabled feature modules as instant experiences using the Play Core Library. When a user downloads and installs your app, the device downloads and installs your app's instant-enabled feature modules, along with the base APK, by default.

7. **dist:title="@string/feature_name"**: Specifies a user-facing title for the module. For instance, the device may show this title when it requests download confirmation. You might need to include the string resource for this title in the base module's module_root/src/source_set/res/values/strings.xml file.

8. **</dist:module>**: Specifies whether to include the module in multi-APKs that target devices running Android 4.4 (API level 20) and lower.

Additionally, in case you apply bundletool to generate APKs from an app bundle, only feature modules that set this property to true are included in the universal APK—which is a monolithic APK that includes code and resources for all device configurations your app supports.

9. **<dist:delivery>**: Used to encapsulate options that customizes module delivery. Please note that each

feature module must configure only one type of these custom delivery options.

10. **<dist:install-time>:** Specifies that the module should be available at install time. This is the default behavior for feature modules that do not specify another type of custom delivery option. It might also specify conditions that limit the module to devices that meet certain requirements, such as device features, user country, or minimum API level.

11. **<dist:removable dist:value="true | false"/>:** When unset or set to false, bundletool will locate install-time modules into the base module when generating split APKs from the bundle. Because there will be fewer split APKs as a result of relocation, this setting may advance your app's performance a little.

    However, when removable is set to true: Install-time modules will not be placed into the base module. You should set it to true only if you want to uninstall modules in the future. But at the same time, configuring too many modules to be removable might increase the install time for your app.

    At times when it defaults to false, it is necessary to set this value in the manifest if you want to disable relocation for a feature module. Yet keep in mind that this feature is only available when using Android Gradle plugin 4.2 or when using bundletool v1.0 from the command line.

12. **<dist:on-demand/>:** Specifies that the module should be available as an on-demand download. That is, the

module is not available at install time, but your app may need to download it later.

In this chapter, you learned how to install and get your development environment ready for Android Studio configuration process. We also showed you how to apply Gradle Build Scripts and launch and navigate Android Studio projects. You should now have the foundation required to be able to review and analyze Android Studio User Interface with its specific Terms, various Folders, Layouts, and Strings.

CHAPTER 3

Android Studio Basics

IN THIS CHAPTER

> ➢ Getting to know Android Studio User Interface components

> ➢ Learning how to control and configure main objects

> ➢ Reviewing the hierarchy of various layouts and widgets

We learned Android Studio installation and configuration process in the previous chapter, reviewed Gradle Build Scripts, and worked with Projects. In this chapter, we will go through Android Studio User Interface (UI) basics and interact with its main components and widgets.

DOI: 10.1201/9781003229070-3

85

Android Studio could be described as a standard windowed environment. In order to make the best use of limited screen real-estate, and to keep you from being confused, Android Studio displays only a small fraction of all the available information at any given time. Some of these content area items are context-sensitive and appear only when the context is appropriate, while others remain hidden until you set to show them, or conversely remain visible until you set to hide them. Therefore, to be able to take full advantage of Android Studio, it is necessary that you understand the functions of these interactive application basics, as well as how and when to display them. In this chapter, we are going to show you how to manage folders, layouts, strings, and views within Android Studio.

ANDROID STUDIO UI

A standard UI of Android Studio consists of an action bar and the application content area. The action bar, typically referred to as the Main Action Bar regulates the view and content area control. Understanding of screen components starts with the basic unit of the android application which is the activity. A UI is defined in an XML file, and during compilation, each item in the XML is compiled into an equivalent Android Graphical User Interface (GUI) class with attributes represented by methods.

Each activity consists of views. A view here stands for a widget that appears on the screen. One or more views can be grouped together into one GroupView. A typical example of ViewGroup is layouts.

When it comes to layouts, you need to know which type you are dealing with. There are many types of layouts. Some of which include: linear, absolute, table, frame, and relative layout. We shall talk about layouts in detail in the following section of this chapter.

Apart from the above-mentioned attributes, there are other attributes that are common in all views and ViewGroups. They could be listed in the following order:

1. **layout_width:** Specifies the width of the View or ViewGroup.

2. **layout_height:** Specifies the height of the View or ViewGroup.

3. **layout_marginTop:** Specifies extra space on the top side of the View or ViewGroup.

4. **layout_marginBottom:** Specifies extra space on the bottom side of the View or ViewGroup.

5. **layout_marginLeft:** Specifies extra space on the left side of the View or ViewGroup.

6. **layout_marginRight:** Specifies extra space on the right side of the View or ViewGroup.

7. **layout_gravity:** Specifies how child Views are positioned.

8. **layout_weight:** Specifies how much of the extra space in the layout should be allocated to the View.

When considering units of measurement and attempting to specify the size of any element on an Android UI, you should keep in mind the following units of dimensional estimate:

1. **DP:** Density-independent pixel. 1 dp in Android Studio is equivalent to one pixel on a 160 dpi screen.

2. **sp:** Scale-independent pixel. This is similar to dp and is recommended for specifying font sizes in Android Studio.

3. **pt:** Point. A point is defined to be 1/72 of an inch, based on the physical screen size.

4. **px:** Pixel. Corresponds to actual pixels on the screen.

As for Screen Densities, even though Android does not use a direct pixel mapping, it uses a handful of quantized Density Independent Pixel values then scales to the actual screen size:

1. **Low density (ldpi):** 120 dpi

2. **Medium density (mdpi):** 160 dpi

3. **High density (hdpi):** 240 dpi

4. **Extra high density (xhdpi):** 320 dpi

TERMS AND FOLDERS

Going back to the action bar, it should still be viewed as one of the most important design elements in your app's activities, since it provides a visual structure and interactive elements required by users. Using the app bar makes your app consistent with other Android apps, allowing users to quickly understand how to work around your app and have a smooth experience. The key functions of the action bar include the following:

- A suitable space for giving your app an identity and indicating the user's location in the app

- Providing access to important actions in a suitable way, such as navigation

- Supporting view switching using tabs or drop-down lists

Action Bar is the element located at the top of the activity screen. It is a prominent feature of a mobile application that has a consistent presence over all its activities. It provides a visual architecture to the app and contains some of the frequently used elements for the users. Android Action Bar was launched by Google in 2013 with the release of Android 3.0(API 11). Before that, this topmost visual element was called AppBar. At that time, it used to hold only the name of the application or current activity. It was not very useful for the users, and developers were looking for options to customize it.

Along with the Action bar, Google includes a support library that is a part of AppCompat which purpose is to provide backward compatibility for older versions of Android and to operate tabbed interfaces. All applications that use the default theme provided by the Android (project name is – Theme.AppCompat.Light.DarkActionBar), contains an Action Bar by default. However, developers can modify it in several ways depending upon their requirements. Components included in the Action Bar are:

- **App Icon:** Displays the branding logo/icon of the application.

- **View Controls:** Section that displays the name of the application or current activity. You can also include spinner or tabbed navigation for switching between views here.

- **Action Button:** This contains some important actions/elements of the app that may be required of you frequently.

- **Action Overflow:** Includes other actions that will be displayed as a menu.

For every menu item, the following attributes could be configured for advanced applicability:

- **android:title:** Its value includes the title of the menu item that will be displayed when a user clicks and holds that item in the app.

- **android:id:** A unique ID for the menu item that will be applied to access it anywhere in the whole application files.

- **android:orderInCategory:** The value of this attribute specify the item's position in the ActionBar. There are two ways to determine the position of different menu items. The first one is to provide the same value of this attribute for all items, and the position will be defined in the same order as they are scripted in the code. The second way is to provide a different numeric value for all items, and then the items will place themselves according to ascending order of this attribute's value.

- **app:showAsAction:** This attribute determines how the item is going to be present in the action bar.

- **android:icon:** The icon of an item is referenced in the drawable directories through this attribute.

In addition to the above-mentioned attributes, there are four possible flag-actions to apply to Action Bar components:

1. **always:** Selecting to display the item in the Action Bar all the time.

2. **ifRoom:** Keeping the item if space is available.

3. **never:** With this flag, the item will not be displayed as an icon in Action Bar, but will be placed in the overflow menu.

4. **withText:** To represent an item as both icon and the title, you may also replace this flag with the always or ifRoom flag (always|withText or ifRoom|withText).

Action Bar has many advantages. First, it acts as a great customized area to build the identity of an app. It also keeps track of the most frequently used actions and makes sure to specify the location of the user in the app. On the other hand, not all features of the Action Bar are introduced at once but took rather long with the release of different API levels such as API 15, 17, and 19. At the same time, the Action Bar tends to behave differently when it runs on different API levels, and the features that were introduced with a particular API do not provide backward compatibility.

Splitting the Action Bar

Since the action items share the action bar real estate with the app icon and title, you might need to split the action bar so that the action elements move to the bottom of the screen. This will give them more space, and thus more elements will be available to the user. However, if there is enough space, for example on larger screens or in landscape mode, the action bar cannot be split.

In order to split the action bar, simply add android:ui Options="splitActionBarWhenNarrow" to each activity in your manifest file that you need to have a split action bar. Yet keep in mind that this only supports API level 14 and above. If you need to add support for lower levels, you should use the following meta-data element:[1]

```
<activity
  android:name="com.example.actionbar.
MainActivity"
```

---

[1] https://www.sitepoint.com/better-user-interfaces-android-action-bar/, Site Point

```
android:label="@string/app_name"
android:uiOptions="splitActionBarWhenNar
row" >
  <meta-data android:name="android.support.
  UI_OPTIONS"
    android:value="splitActionBarWhenNar
    row" />
  <intent-filter>
    <action android:name="android.intent.
    action.MAIN" />
    <category android:name="android.intent.
    category.LAUNCHER" />
  </intent-filter>
</activity>
```

Hiding the Action Bar

There are instances when you do not want to have the action bar visible at all times. A common example of this is the Gallery app, which hides the action bar when the user is looking at an image and shows the action bar when they touch the image. To modify action bar visibility on touch, insert the following feature to your activity file:[2]

```
@Override
public boolean onTouchEvent(MotionEvent
event) {
  if(event.getAction() == MotionEvent.
ACTION_DOWN) {
    toggleActionBar();
  }
  return true;
}
```

---

[2] https://www.sitepoint.com/better-user-interfaces-android-action-bar/, Site Point

```
private void toggleActionBar() {
  ActionBar actionBar = getActionBar();

  if(actionBar != null) {
    if(actionBar.isShowing()) {
      actionBar.hide();
    }
    else {
      actionBar.show();
    }
  }
}
```

Please note that it is possible to show/hide the action bar by tapping the screen while running the application. You might also notice that the content on the screen changes position with each show/hide. This is because when you hide/show the action bar, the activity resizes, affecting the content's size and position. In order to prevent this, it is recommended to overlay the action bar as described next.

Overlaying the Action Bar

Overlaying the action bar provides a better hide/show occurrence since the activity does not resize on each hide/show, letting your content to stay put. You can enable overlaying by setting android:windowActionBarOverlay to true in your theme file, which should be the Theme.Holo theme or one of its descendants. In res/values/styles.xml, insert the following:[3]

---

[3] https://www.sitepoint.com/better-user-interfaces-android-action-bar/, Site point

```
<resources>
  <style name="AppBaseTheme"
parent="android:Theme.Light">
</style>

<!-- Application theme. -->
<style name="AppTheme"
parent="AppBaseTheme">
    <item name="android:windowActionBarOve
rlay">true</item>
  </style>
</resources>
```

Once you activate the application, you should be able to notice that the content on the screen does not change position regardless of the action bar being hidden or revealed.

To summarize this section, the action bar is an important design element, and it should be mastered to greatly improve an app's user experience. Here, we have looked at some basic configurations you can use on the action bar for your app's UI, but keep in mind that there are more out there to learn once you are ready for it.

LAYOUTS

Android Layout is used to define the UI that holds the UI controls or widgets that are displayed on the screen of your application or activity screen. As a general rule, every application is a combination of View and ViewGroup. And as we already stated, an android application contains a large number of activities, and we can treat each activity as one page of the application. Meaning, each activity contains multiple UI components, and those components are the instances of the View and ViewGroup. All the elements that you see in a layout are built using a hierarchy of View and ViewGroup objects.

A View could also be defined as the UI which is necessary to create interactive UI components such as TextView, ImageView, EditText, or a RadioButton. In addition, it is also responsible for event handling and drawing.

A ViewGroup would then be a base class for layouts and layouts parameters that contain other Views or ViewGroups as well as define the layout properties. The Android framework typically allows users to use UI elements or widgets in two ways: When building the XML file or when dynamically creating elements in the Kotlin file.

Layout Position

The geometry (shape) of a view is that of a rectangle. A view also has a location, presented as a pair of left and top coordinates, and two dimensions, that come as a width and a height. The unit for location and dimensions is the pixel.

If required, you can retrieve the location of a view by invoking the methods getLeft() and getTop(). The former returns the left, or X, coordinate of the rectangle representing the view. The latter returns the top, or Y, coordinate of the rectangle representing the view. These methods both return the location of the view relative to its parent. To illustrate, when getLeft() returns 20, that means the view is located 20 pixels to the right of the left edge of its direct parent.

Moreover, there are several convenience methods are offered to prevent unnecessary computations, namely GetRight() and getBottom(). These methods return the coordinates of the right and bottom edges of the rectangle representing the view. For example, calling GetRight() would be similar to the following computation: getLeft() + getWidth().

The size of a view is expressed with a width and a height. A view generally has two pairs of width and height values. The first pair is known as measured width and measured height. These dimensions are used to determine how big a view wants to be within its parent. The measured dimensions can be gathered by calling getMeasuredWidth() and getMeasuredHeight().

The second pair is simply known as width and height, or some might call it drawing width and drawing height. These dimensions determine the actual size of the view on screen, at drawing time, and after layout. These values may, but do not necessarily have to, be different from the measured width and height. The width and height can be gathered by calling getWidth() and getHeight().

In order to measure its dimensions, a view has to consider its padding. The padding is expressed in pixels for the left, top, right, and bottom parts of the view. Padding can be applied to offset the content of the view by a specific number of pixels. For example, a left padding of 2 will push the view's content by 2 pixels to the right of the left edge. Thus, padding can be set using the setPadding(int, int, int, int) method and queried by calling getPaddingLeft(), getPaddingTop(), getPaddingRight(), and getPaddingBottom().

It is worth noting that even if a view can define padding, it does not provide any support for margins. Yet such support could be provided using view groups.

Types of Android Layout

As already mentioned, there are different types of Android Layout. The list goes like that:[4]

- **Android Linear Layout:** LinearLayout is a ViewGroup subclass, used to provide child View elements one by one either in a specific direction, either horizontally or vertically based on the orientation property.

- **Android Relative Layout:** RelativeLayout is a ViewGroup subclass, used to specify the position of child View elements relative to each other like (A to the right of B) or relative to the parent (fix to the top of the parent).

- **Android Constraint Layout:** ConstraintLayout is a ViewGroup subclass, used to set the position of layout constraints for every child View relative to other views present. A ConstraintLayout is almost similar to a RelativeLayout, but has more functionality.

- **Android Frame Layout:** FrameLayout is a ViewGroup subclass, used to specify the position of View elements it contains on the top of each other to display only a single View inside the FrameLayout.

- **Android Table Layout:** TableLayout is a ViewGroup subclass, used to display the child View elements in rows and columns.

- **Android Web View:** WebView is a browser that is used to display the web pages in our activity layout.

---

[4] https://developer.android.com/guide/topics/ui/declaring-layout, Android

- **Android ListView:** ListView is a ViewGroup, used to display scrollable lists of items in a single column.

- **Android Grid View:** GridView is a ViewGroup that is used to display a scrollable list of items in a grid view of rows and columns.

Using UI Elements in the XML File

It is possible to create a layout similar to web pages using the XML file. The XML layout file holds at least one root element in which additional layout elements or widgets can be included to build a View hierarchy. Let's take a look at this example:[5]

```
<?xml version="1.0" encoding="utf-8"?>
<LinearLayout
    xmlns:android="http:// schemas.android.
com/apk/res/android"
    xmlns:tools="http:// schemas.android.
com/tools"
    android:orientation="vertical"
    android:layout_width="match_parent"
    android:layout_height="match_parent"
    tools:context=".MainActivity">

    <!--EditText with id editText-->
    <EditText
        android:id="@+id/editText"
        android:layout_width=
"match_parent"
        android:layout_height=
"wrap_content"
```

---

[5] https://www.geeksforgeeks.org/android-ui-layouts/, Geeks for Geeks

```
        android:layout_margin="16dp"
        android:hint="Input"
        android:inputType="text"/>

    <!--Button with id showInput-->
    <Button
        android:id="@+id/showInput"
        android:layout_width=
"wrap_content"
        android:layout_height=
"wrap_content"
        android:layout_gravity=
"center_horizontal"
        android:text="show"
        android:backgroundTint="@color/
colorPrimary"
        android:textColor="@android:color/
white"/>
</LinearLayout>
```

Once you have created the layout, now you need to load the XML layout resource from the activity onCreate() callback method and access the UI element from the XML using findViewById:

```
override fun onCreate(savedInstanceState:
Bundle?) {
        super.onCreate(savedInstanceState)
        setContentView(R.layout.
activity_main)

        // finding the button
        val showButton =
findViewById<Button>(R.id.showInput)
```

```
    // finding the edit text
    val editText =
findViewById<EditText>(R.id.editText)
```

You should observe the above code and see that we are calling our layout using the setContentView method in the form of R.layout.activity_main. Normally, during the launch of our activity, the onCreate() callback method will be retrieved by the android framework to get the required layout for an activity.

Layouts are an essential segment of Android applications that directly affect the user experience. If designed and executed poorly, your layout can lead to a memory-hungry application with slow UIs. The Android SDK has tools to assist you in identifying problems in your layout performance, which will result in smooth scrolling interfaces with a minimum memory footprint once implemented.

It is a common misconception thinking that following the basic layout structures leads to the most efficient layouts. At the same time, each widget and layout you include in your application requires initialization, layout, and drawing. To illustrate with an example, using nested instances of LinearLayout can lead to an excessively deep view hierarchy. Moreover, nesting several instances of LinearLayout that use the layout_weight parameter can be particularly expensive as each child needs to be measured twice. This is particularly important when the layout is inflated repeatedly, such as when used in a ListView or GridView. However, there are certain things you can do to optimize your layout performance:

Inspect Your Layout

The Android SDK has a tool named Hierarchy Viewer that lets you analyze your layout while your application is running. Activating this tool will help you to discover potential issues in the layout performance. The way Hierarchy Viewer works is by allowing you to choose running processes on a connected device or emulator, then present the whole layout tree. The traffic lights on each block represent its Measure, Layout, and Draw performance, letting you identify potential issues.

Revise Your Layout

Because the layout performance might slow down due to a nested LinearLayout, the performance might improve by flattening the layout—making it shallow and wide, rather than narrow and deep. As minor as they might seem, the advantages are multiplied several times because this layout could be applied for almost every activity out there.

Most of the difference is due to the use of layout_weight in the LinearLayout setting, which can slow down the speed of measurement. It is just one example of how each layout has appropriate applications, and you should carefully revise whether using layout weight is absolutely necessary. In some complex layouts, the system may waste effort measuring the same UI element more than once. This concept is called double taxation.

Use Lint

It is always a good idea to run the lint tool on your layout files to see if there are any possible view hierarchy optimizations. Lint has replaced the Layoutopt tool and has much greater functionality for such matters. Yet there are certain lint rules you should be aware of before starting:

- **Use compound drawables:** A LinearLayout that contains an ImageView and a TextView can be more efficiently managed as a compound drawable.

- **Merge root frame:** If a FrameLayout is the root of a layout and does not provide background or padding, it can be replaced with a merge tag which is slightly more efficient.

- **Useless leaf:** A layout that has no children or no background can often be removed for a flatter and more efficient layout hierarchy.

- **Useless parent:** A layout with children that has no siblings and no background can be removed and have its children relocated directly into the parent for a flatter and more efficient layout hierarchy.

- **Deep layouts:** Layouts with too much nesting are a bad influence on overall performance. Consider using flatter layouts such as RelativeLayout or GridLayout to improve performance. The default maximum depth should be at ten.

Another advantage that Lint has is that it is smoothly integrated into Android Studio. Lint automatically runs whenever you compile your program. With Android Studio, you can be sure to run lint inspections for a specific build variant, or for all build variants.

Although Android offers a variety of widgets to provide small and re-usable interactive elements, you might also need to re-use larger items that require a special layout. To efficiently re-use complete layouts, you can use the <include/> and <merge/> tags to include another layout inside the current layout.

Reusing layouts is particularly great as it allows you to create reusable complex layouts. For instance, a yes/no button panel, or a custom progress bar with description text. It also means that any elements of your application that are common across multiple layouts can be extracted and administered separately before combining them into a single layout. So while you can create individual UI components by writing a custom View, you can also easily do it by re-using a layout file.

Creating a Re-Usable Layout
If you already have the layout that you want to re-use in mind, start by creating a new XML file and defining the

layout. For example, let's take a layout that defines a title bar to be included in each activity (titlebar.xml):[6]

```
<FrameLayout xmlns:android="http://schemas.
android.com/apk/res/android"
    xmlns:tools="http://schemas.android.
com/tools"
    android:layout_width="match_parent"
    android:layout_height="wrap_content"
    android:background="@color/
titlebar_bg"
    tools:showIn="@layout/activity_main" >

    <ImageView android:layout_width=
"wrap_content"
               android:layout_height=
"wrap_content"
               android:src="@drawable/
gafricalogo" />
</FrameLayout>
```

Now, the root View should be displayed exactly how you would like it in each activity segment to which you add this layout.

Also keep in mind that the tools:showIn attribute in the XML above is a special attribute that is removed during compilation and retrieved only at design time in Android Studio—It identifies a layout that includes this file, so you can review and modify this file as it emerges while embedded in a parent layout.

---

[6] https://developer.android.com/training/improving-layouts/reusing-layouts, Android

Use the <include> Tag

It is also recommended to add the <include/> tag inside the layout to which you want to add the reusable component. To demonstrate, take a look at a layout that includes the title bar from above:[7]

```
<LinearLayout xmlns:android="http://
schemas.android.com/apk/res/android"
    android:orientation="vertical"
    android:layout_width="match_parent"
    android:layout_height="match_parent"
    android:background="@color/app_bg"
    android:gravity="center_horizontal">
```

Now, include the <include layout="@layout/titlebar"/>

```
    <TextView android:layout_width=
"match_parent"
            android:layout_height=
"wrap_content"
            android:text="@string/hello"
            android:padding="10dp" />
</LinearLayout>
```

It is also possible to override all the layout parameters (any android:layout_* attributes) of the included layout's root view by inserting them in the <include/> tag. For instance:

```
<include android:id="@+id/news_title"
        android:layout_width=
"match_parent"
```

---

[7] https://developer.android.com/training/improving-layouts/reusing-layouts, Android

```
        android:layout_height=
"match_parent"
        layout="@layout/title"/>
```

At the same time, if you need to override layout attributes using the <include> tag, you must override both android:layout_height and android:layout_width for other layout attributes to be activated.

Use the <merge> Tag

The <merge /> is a great solution when you need to eliminate redundant view groups in your view hierarchy when inserting one layout within another. To be precise, if your main layout is a vertical LinearLayout in which two consecutive views can be re-used in multiple layouts, then the re-usable layout in which you set the two views requires its own root view. Nevertheless, using another LinearLayout as the root for the re-usable layout would turn into a vertical LinearLayout inside a vertical LinearLayout. The nested LinearLayout serves no other purpose than to slow down your UI performance.

To avoid adding such a redundant view group, you can use the following <merge> element as the root view for the re-usable layout:[8]

```
<merge xmlns:android="http://schemas.
android.com/apk/res/android">
    <Button
        android:layout_width="fill_parent"
```

---

[8] https://developer.android.com/training/improving-layouts/reusing-layouts, Android

```
        android:layout_height=
"wrap_content"
        android:text="@string/add"/>

    <Button
        android:layout_width="fill_parent"
        android:layout_height=
"wrap_content"
        android:text="@string/delete"/>
</merge>
```

Now, if you include this layout in another layout (using the <include/> tag), the system will simply omit the <merge> element and place the two buttons directly in the layout, instead of the <include/> tag.

STRINGS

A string element provides text strings for your application with additional text styling and formatting. There are three main types of strings that you can use in Android Studio:

- **String:** Identified as an XML resource that provides a single string.

- **String Array:** Stands for an XML resource that provides an array of strings.

- **Quantity Strings (Plurals):** XML resource that carries different strings for pluralization.

In case you are wondering, all three strings styles are capable of applying some styling markup and formatting arguments. Now let's take a closer look at each string type.

String

A single string can be referenced from the application as well as from other resource files such as an XML layout. It is considered to be a simple element that is referenced using the value provided in the name attribute. It is also possible to combine string resources with other simple resources in one XML file, under one <resources> element.

The typical file location is at: res/values/filename.xml

The filename is arbitrary as the <string> element's name would later be used as the resource ID.

Standard resource references are:[9]

In Java: R.string.string_name

In XML:@string/string_name

The syntax to apply for a string is:

```
<?xml version="1.0" encoding="utf-8"?>
<resources>
    <string
        name="string_name"
        >text_string</string>
</resources>
```

When it comes to the syntax elements, please note that:

<resources> – is a required feature that must be the root node, without attributes.

<string> – can include styling tags but not apostrophes or quotation marks.

---

[9] https://developer.android.com/guide/topics/resources/string-resource, Android

String Array

An array of strings can too be referenced from the application and be perceived as a simple resource that runs using the value provided in the name attribute. In addition, you can combine string array resources with other simple resources in one XML file, under one <resources> element.

Standard file location is at: res/values/filename.xml

The filename is also arbitrary and the <string-array> element's name will later be used as the resource ID.

The resource reference in Java is: R.array.string_array_name

Generic syntax to apply is:

```xml
<?xml version="1.0" encoding="utf-8"?>
<resources>
    <string-array
        name="string_array_name">
        <item
            >text_string</item>
    </string-array>
</resources>
```

Here, a string array can include styling tags as well as refer to another string resource in case it is a child of <string-array> element. However, you should still avoid using apostrophes or quotation marks.

Quantity Strings (Plurals)

Normally, different languages have different rules for grammatical arrangements with quantity. In English, for instance, the quantity 1 is a special case. You can write "1 apple," but for any other quantity you would have to write "n apples." This difference between singular and plural is very usual, yet you have many other languages that have their own distinctions and peculiarities. The ordinary set supported by Android is zero, one, two, few, many, and other.

The rules for deciding which case to use for a given language and quantity can be very confusing at first. That is why Android provides you with methods such as getQuantityString() to select the appropriate resource for you.

Even if it is called "quantity strings," technically quantity strings should only be used for plurals. It would not work out if you apply quantity strings to implement something like Gmail's "Inbox" versus "Inbox (12)" when there are unread messages, for instance. It might seem suitable to use quantity strings instead of an if statement, but it is important to remember that some languages (such as Chinese) do not have these grammatical distinctions at all, so you will always get the other string.

The decision of which string to use has to be made mostly based on grammatical necessity. To illustrate, in English, a string for zero is omitted even if the quantity is 0, because 0 is not grammatically different from 2, or any other number except 1 ("zero apples," "one apple," "two apples," etc.). On the other hand, in Korean, for example, only the other string is ever used. It is important not to be misguided either by the fact that two sounds like it could only apply to the quantity 2: A language may require that 2, 12, 101 are all treated equally to each other but different to other quantities. Here, the best you can do is rely on your translator to find out what distinctions foreign languages actually insist upon.

Sometimes it is possible to avoid quantity strings at all by using quantity-neutral formulations such as "Apples: 1." This could potentially make your application and your translators' work easier if it is an acceptable style for your end product.

To summarize, plurals collection is a simple resource that is referenced using the value provided in the name attribute. Additionally, it is also possible to merge plurals resources with other simple resources in one XML file, under one <resources> element.

Standard file location is at: res/values/filename.xml

The filename here is arbitrary as the element's name will later be used as the resource ID.

Resource reference in Java is: R.plurals.plural_name

Generated syntax to apply is:[10]

```
<?xml version="1.0" encoding="utf-8"?>
<resources>
    <plurals
        name="plural_name">
        <item
            quantity=["zero" | "one" |
"two" | "few" | "many" | "other"]
            >text_string</item>
    </plurals>
</resources>
```

---

[10] https://developer.android.com/guide/topics/resources/string-resource, Android

At the same time, when you use this type of string, make sure to add indicators showing its value. Valid values, with non-exhaustive examples in parentheses, include the following:

1. **Zero:** Applies when the language requires special treatment of the number 0 (as in Arabic).

2. **One:** Applies when the language needs special treatment of numbers like one (as with the number 1 in English or in Russian with any number ending in 1 but not ending in 11).

3. **Two:** Applies when the language requires special treatment of numbers like two (as with 2 in Welsh, or 102 in Slovenian).

4. **Few:** Applies when the language requires special treatment of "small" numbers (as with 2, 3, and 4 in Czech; or numbers ending 2, 3, or 4 but not 12, 13, or 14 in Polish).

5. **Many:** Applies when the language requires special treatment of "large" numbers (as with numbers ending 11–99 in Maltese).

6. **Other:** Applies when the language does not require special treatment of the given quantity (as with all numbers in Chinese, or 42 in English).

There are also a few important things one should learn about how to properly format and style string resources:

Handling Special Characters
When a string holds characters that have special usage in XML, you should omit the characters according to the

standard XML/HTML escaping rules. In such cases when you need to escape a character that has special meaning in Android you may insert a preceding backslash.

By default, Android combines sequences of whitespace characters into a single space. You can prevent this by enclosing the relevant part of your string in double-quotes. In this case, all whitespace characters (including newlines) will stay unedited within the quoted region. Double quotes will let you use regular single unescaped quotes as well. Standard escaped forms include the following:

Character	Escaped Form(s)
@	\@
?	\?
New line	\n
Tab	\t
U+XXXX Unicode character	\uXXXX
Single quote (')	\'
Double quote (")	\"

At times you might have to deal with cases of whitespace collapsing and Android escaping after your resource file gets parsed as XML. This simply means that <string> &#30; ̾ Ϳ</string> (space, punctuation space, Unicode Em space) all collapse to a single space (" "), because they are all Unicode spaces after the file is parsed as an XML. In order to preserve those spaces as they are, you can either quote them (<string>" &#30; ̾ Ϳ"</string>) or use Android escaping (<string> \u0030 \u830 \u895</string>).

However, from XML parser's perspective, there is no difference between <string>"Test this"</string> and <string>"Test this"</string> at all. Both forms will not display any quotes but activate Android whitespace-preserving quoting that will have no practical impact in this case.

Formatting Strings

In case you need to format your strings, then you can do so by placing your format arguments in the string resource, as illustrated by the following example:

```
<string name="welcome_messages">Hello,
%1$s! You have %2$d new messages.</string>
```

In this example, the format string has two arguments: %1$s is a string and %2$d is a decimal number. Here, you need to format the string by calling getString(int, Object…). For example:

```
var text = getString(R.string.welcome_
messages, username, mailCount)
```

It is also possible to add styling to your strings with HTML markup. For example:

```
<?xml version="1.0" encoding="utf-8"?>
<resources>
    <string name="welcome">Welcome to
<b>Android</b>!</string>
</resources>
```

You can make use of the following HTML elements that are supported:

1. **Bold:** <b>, <em>

2. **Italic:** <i>, <cite>, <dfn>

3. **25% larger text:** <big>

4. **20% smaller text:** <small>

5. **Setting font properties:** <font face="font_family" color="hex_color">. Examples of possible font families include monospace, serif, and sans_serif.

6. **Setting a monospace font family:** <tt>

7. **Strikethrough:** <s>, <strike>, <del>

8. **Underline:** <u>

9. **Superscript:** <sup>

10. **Subscript:** <sub>

11. **Bullet points:** <ul>, <li>

12. **Line breaks:**

13. **Division:** <div>

14. **CSS style:** <span style="color|background_color|text-decoration">

15. **Paragraphs:** <p dir="rtl | ltr" style="…">

However, if you do not need to apply formatting, you can set TextView text directly by calling setText(java.lang.CharSequence). If you might occasionally need to create a styled text resource that is also used as a format string, you should do so by writing the HTML tags with escaped entities, which are then recovered with fromHtml(String), after the formatting takes place. For example:[11]

---

[11] https://developer.android.com/guide/topics/resources/string-resource, Android

Start by storing your styled text resource as an HTML-escaped string:

```
<resources>
  <string name="welcome_messages">Hello,
%1$s! You have &lt;b>%2$d new messages&lt;
/b>.</string>
</resources>
```

Then format the string as usual, but also call fromHtml (String) to convert the HTML text into styled text:

```
val text: String = getString(R.string.
welcome_messages, username, mailCount)
val styledText: Spanned = Html.
fromHtml(text, FROM_HTML_MODE_LEGACY)
```

Because the fromHtml(String) method formats all HTML entities, make sure to escape any possible HTML characters in the strings you use with the formatted text, using htmlEncode(String). For example, if you are formatting a string that has characters such as "<" or "&," then they must be escaped before formatting, so that when the formatted string goes through fromHtml(String), the characters come out the way they were originally scripted. To illustrate with an example:

```
val escapedUsername: String = TextUtils.
htmlEncode(username)
val text: String = getString(R.string.
welcome_messages, escapedUsername,
mailCount)
val styledText: Spanned = Html.
fromHtml(text, FROM_HTML_MODE_LEGACY)
```

VIEWS

Android offers a sophisticated and greatly componentized model for building your UI, based on the fundamental layout classes: View and ViewGroup. We have already gone through a variety of prebuilt View and ViewGroup subclasses—called widgets and layouts, respectively—that you can utilize to construct your UI.

A partial list of available widgets that we have mentioned included Button, TextView, EditText, ListView, CheckBox, RadioButton, Gallery, Spinner, and the more special-purpose AutoCompleteTextView, ImageSwitcher, and TextSwitcher. Among the layouts available are LinearLayout, FrameLayout, RelativeLayout, and others.

In case you find yourself in a situation where none of the prebuilt widgets or layouts meets your needs, you can always create your own View subclass. If you only need to make small adjustments to an existing widget or layout, you can simply subclass the widget or layout and override its methods.

Creating your own View subclasses gives you precise power over the appearance and function of all the screen components. To give you a vague idea of the authority you get with custom views, here are some examples of what you could potentially do with them:

- You could create a completely custom-rendered View type or a total volume control using 2D graphics that resemble an analog electronic control.

- You could combine a group of View elements into a new single component, in order to make something like a ComboBox (a combination of popup list and free entry text field), or a dual-pane selector control (left and right pane with a list in each where you can reassign which item is in which list).

- You could modify the way that an EditText component appears on the screen (the Notepad Tutorial uses this to good effect to create a lined notepad page).

- You should also be able to capture other events like key presses and handle them in some custom way (such as for a game).

Now, let's see some working approaches to creating custom Views and using them in your application.

The Basic Approach

Here is a brief overview of what you need to know to get started in creating your own View components:

First, extend an existing View class or subclass with your own class. Make sure to override some of the methods from the superclass. The superclass methods to override start with "on," for instance, onDraw(), onMeasure(), and onKeyDown(). These are the same ones you use for the events in Activity or ListActivity that you override for lifecycle and other functionality settings.

Then, you should be using your new extension class. Once completed, your new extension class can be applied in place of the view upon which it was based. In addition, the same extension classes can be defined as inner classes inside the activities that use them. This is beneficial because it controls access to them but at the same time is not absolutely necessary (might be in case you want to create a new public View for wider use in your application).

Fully Customized Components

Fully customized components can be used to create graphical components that appear whenever and in whatever shaper and form you decide. You might want a graphical Volume Unit meter that looks like an old analog gauge, or a sing-a-long text view so you can sing along with a karaoke machine. Either way, standard built-in components cannot deliver that, no matter how you combine them.

However, you can easily create components that look and function in any way you like, limited perhaps only by your imagination, the size of the screen, and the available operation power (Keep in mind that your application might have to run on something with significantly less power than your desktop workstation).

In order to create a fully customized component:

You usually have to start by extending the View to create your new super component. You can supply a constructor which can take attributes and parameters from the XML, and you can also set your own parameters (perhaps the color, range, or width).

You then would probably want to create your own event listeners, property accessors and modifiers, and possibly more sophisticated functioning of your component class as well. In such a case, you will almost certainly have to override onMeasure() and are also likely to need to override onDraw() if you want the component to show something. While both have default behavior, the default onDraw() will do nothing, and the default onMeasure() will always set a size of 100 × 100—which is not the most desired option.

Extend onDraw() and onMeasure()

The onDraw() method acts as a canvas upon which you can implement anything you need: 2D graphics, other standard or custom-made components, styled text, or anything else you might require for the project. On a side note, keep in mind that this does not extend to 3D graphics. If you need to use 3D graphics, you must extend SurfaceView instead of View, and draw from a separate thread.

onMeasure() should be perceived as a critical piece of the rendering contract between your component and its container. onMeasure() should be modified to efficiently and appropriately report the measurements of its contained parts. This is made slightly more complicated by the requirements of limits from the parent (which are passed in to the onMeasure() method) and by the requirement to call the setMeasuredDimension() method with the measured width and height once they have been computed. In case you fail to call this method from an overridden onMeasure() method, the outcome will be an exception at measurement time.

At a high level, implementing onMeasure() should go the following way: The overridden onMeasure() method is called with width and height measure details (widthMeasureSpec and heightMeasureSpec parameters, both are integer codes representing dimensions) which should be treated as requirements for the restrictions on the width and height measurements you should put together.

Your component's onMeasure() method should estimate a measurement width and height which will be required to render the component. It should try to stay within the specifications passed in, although it can potentially exceed them (in this case, the parent can decide what to do, including clipping, scrolling, throwing an exception, or asking the onMeasure() to try again, using different measurement specifications).

Once the width and height are set, the setMeasured Dimension(int width, int height) method must be invoked with the calculated measurements. If this step is omitted, the exception could be thrown. The summary of some of the standard methods that the framework calls on views are in Table 3.1.[12]

In case you are not looking to create a completely customized component, but instead are looking to put together a reusable component that holds a group of existing controls, then creating a Compound Component (or Compound Control) might be the perfect option. To put it simply, this brings together a number of more independent controls (or views) into a logical group of items that can be executed as a single thing. To illustrate, a Combo Box can be thought of as a combination of a single line EditText field with an attached PopupList. If you press the button and choose something from the list, it fills the EditText field, but also letting the user type something directly into the EditText.

In Android, there are actually two other Views readily available to do this: Spinner and AutoCompleteTextView, but regardless, the concept of a Combo Box seems to be the simplest example for this case.

---

[12] https://developer.android.com/guide/topics/ui/custom-components? hl=hi&skip_cache=true, Android

TABLE 3.1 Standard Methods and Their Definitions

Category	Methods	Description
Creation	Constructors	A form of the constructor is called when the view is created from code and a form is called when the view is inflated from a layout file. The second form should parse and apply any attributes defined in the layout file.
	onFinishInflate()	Called after a view and all of its children have been inflated from XML.
Layout	onMeasure(int, int)	Called to determine the size requirements for this view and all of its children.
	onLayout(boolean, int, int, int, int)	Called when this view should assign a size and position to all of its children.
	onSizeChanged(int, int, int, int)	Called when the size of this view has changed.
Drawing	onDraw(Canvas)	Called when the view should render its content.
Event processing	onKeyDown(int, KeyEvent)	Called when a new key event occurs.
	onKeyUp(int, KeyEvent)	Called when a key up event occurs.
	onTrackballEvent(MotionEvent)	Called when a trackball motion event occurs.
	onTouchEvent(MotionEvent)	Called when a touch screen motion event occurs.
Focus	onFocusChanged(boolean, int, Rect)	Called when the view gains or loses focus.
	onWindowFocusChanged(boolean)	Called when the window containing the view gains or loses focus.
Attaching	onAttachedToWindow()	Called when the view is attached to a window.
	onDetachedFromWindow()	Called when the view is detached from its window.
	onWindowVisibilityChanged(int)	Called when the visibility of the window containing the view has changed.

In order to create a compound component:

The usual starting point is a Layout, so you should create a class that extends a Layout. Perhaps in the case of a Combo box, you might use a LinearLayout with horizontal orientation. At the same time, since other layouts can be nested inside, the compound component can be arbitrarily complex and overly structured. Yet just like with an Activity, you can use either the declarative (XML-based) method of creating the contained components, or you can nest them programmatically from your code.

In the constructor for the new class, you can take whatever parameters the superclass requires, and pass them through to the superclass constructor first. Then you should set up the other views to use within your new component where you would create the EditText field and the PopupList. Here you can also introduce your own attributes and parameters into the XML that can be later invoked and used by your constructor.

In addition, it is also allowed to create listeners for events that your contained views might generate, for instance, a listener method for the List Item Click Listener to update the contents of the EditText if a list selection is made.

To sum up, the use of a Layout as the basis for a Custom Control has a number of advantages, including:

- You can specify the layout using the declarative XML files similar to the activity screen, or you can create views programmatically and nest them into the layout from your code.

- The onDraw() and onMeasure() methods will most likely have suitable functionality, so you do not have to modify them.

- At last, you can very quickly design arbitrarily complex compound views and re-apply them later as if they were a single component.

A well-designed custom view should be treated like any other well-designed class. It combines a specific set of functionality with a friendly UI and extensive memory size. In addition to being a well-designed class, a custom view is expected to: Conform to Android standards, provide custom attributes that work with Android XML layouts, send accessibility events, and be compatible with multiple Android platforms.

The Android framework provides a set of base classes and XML tags to encourage you to create a view that meets all of these demands. Now let's discuss how to use the Android framework to create the core functionality of a subclass view.

Subclass a View

All of the view classes included in the Android framework extend View. Your custom view can also extend View directly, or you can save resources by extending one of the existing view subclasses, such as Button.

In order to allow Android Studio to correspond to your view, at a minimum you should provide a constructor that takes a Context and an AttributeSet object as parameters. This constructor allows the layout editor to produce and edit an instance of your view, for instance, class PieChart(context: Context, attrs: AttributeSet): View(context, attrs).

Define Custom Attributes

In order to add a built-in View to your UI, you need to specify it in an XML element and regulate its appearance and functionality with element attributes. Well-written custom views can also be added and styled via XML. To enable this capability in your custom view, you should:

- Define custom attributes for your view in a <declare-styleable> resource element

- Identify values for the attributes in your XML layout

- Retrieve attribute values at runtime

- Apply the retrieved attribute values to your view

To define custom attributes, insert <declare-styleable> resources into your project. It is quite usual to put these resources into a res/values/attrs.xml file. Take a look at this example of an attrs.xml file:[13]

```
<resources>
    <declare-styleable name="PieChart">
        <attr name="showText"
format="boolean" />
        <attr name="labelPosition"
format="enum">
            <enum name="left" value="0"/>
```

---

[13] https://developer.android.com/guide/topics/ui/custom-components? hl=hi&skip_cache=true, Android

```
            <enum name="right" value="1"/>
        </attr>
    </declare-styleable>
</resources>
```

This code defines two main attributes, showText and label-Position, that belong to a styleable entity named PieChart. The name of the styleable entity is the same name as the title of the class that defines the custom view, and even though it is not strictly necessary to follow this arrangement, many popular code editors still use this naming convention to enable statement completion.

Once you have defined the custom attributes, you can use them in layout XML files just like built-in attributes. The only difference is that your custom attributes would be located in a different namespace. Instead of staying at the http://schemas.android.com/apk/res/android namespace, they would be at http://schemas.android.com/apk/res/[your package name]. To demonstrate, let's take a look at these PieChart attributes:[14]

```
<?xml version="1.0" encoding="utf-8"?>
<LinearLayout xmlns:android="http://
schemas.android.com/apk/res/android"
    xmlns:custom="http://schemas.android.
com/apk/res/com.example.customviews">
 <com.example.customviews.charting.PieChart
      custom:showText="true"
      custom:labelPosition="left" />
</LinearLayout>
```

---

[14] https://developer.android.com/guide/topics/ui/custom-components?
hl=hi&skip_cache=true, Android

In case you want to avoid having to repeat the long namespace URI, you can make use of the xmlns directive. This directive assigns the alias custom to the namespace http://schemas.android.com/apk/res/com.example.customviews and lets you choose any alias you need for your namespace.

Also, see the name of the XML tag that includes the custom view to the layout. It is the fully qualified name of the custom view class. And if your view class is an inner class, you should further qualify it with the name of the view's outer class. For example, the above PieChart class has an inner class called PieView. In order to use the custom attributes from this class, you should use the tag com.example. custom views.charting.PieChart$PieView.

Apply Custom Attributes

When a view is created from an XML layout, all of the attributes in the XML tag are retrieved from the resource bundle and directed into the view's constructor as an AttributeSet. Even though it is possible to read values from the AttributeSet directly, doing so has some drawbacks like resource references within attribute values will not be fully resolved, and styles are not normally applied to it.

What you can do instead is pass the AttributeSet to obtainStyledAttributes(). This method will deliver a TypedArray array of values that have already been dereferenced and styled.

The Android resource compiler actually does a lot of work for you to access obtainStyledAttributes() easier.

Thus, for each <declare-styleable> resource in the res directory, the generated R.java determines both an array of attribute ids and a set of constants that define the index for each attribute in the array. You can use the predefined constants to read the attributes from the TypedArray. Here's how the above mentioned PieChart class reads its attributes:

```
init {
    context.theme.obtainStyledAttributes(
            attrs,
            R.styleable.PieChart,
            0, 0).apply {
              try {
            mShowText = getBoolean
(R.styleable.PieChart_showText, false)
            textPos = getInteger
(R.styleable.PieChart_labelPosition, 0)
        } finally {
            recycle()
        }
    }
}
```

In addition, keep in mind that since TypedArray objects are a shared resource, they must be recycled after use.

Add Properties and Events

Attributes are a great way of regulating the behavior and appearance of views, yet they can only be read when the view is initialized. In order to establish dynamic tendency, you may try exposing a property getter and setter pair for each custom attribute. The following snippet illustrates how PieChart exposes a property called showText:

```
fun isShowText(): Boolean {
    return mShowText
}
fun setShowText(showText: Boolean) {
    mShowText = showText
    invalidate()
    requestLayout()
}
```

Here, remember that setShowText calls both invalidate() and requestLayout() features. These calls are important to ensure that the view is stable. You might need to invalidate the view after imposing any change to its properties that might change its appearance so that the system gets the signal that it needs to be redrawn. Similarly, you need to request a new layout if a property introduces changes that might affect the size or shape of the view. Forgetting these method calls can cause hard-to-find bugs in the system.

Moreover, custom views should also support event listeners to transmit important events. For example, PieChart exposes a custom event called OnCurrentItemChanged to notify listeners that the user has modified the pie chart to focus on a new pie slice.

It might be easy to forget to expose properties and events, especially if you are the only user of the custom view. However, taking some time to carefully determine your view's interface will significantly reduce any future maintenance costs. A good piece of advice to take into consideration is to always expose any property that impacts the visible appearance or behavior of your custom view.

Design for Accessibility

It is also important for your custom view to support the widest range of users. This also includes users with disabilities that prevent them from seeing or using a touchscreen. In order to support users with disabilities, it is highly recommended to:

- Mark your input fields using the android: contentDescription attribute

- Send accessibility events by calling sendAccessibilityEvent() when appropriate

- Support alternative controllers, such as D-pad and trackball

With such a well-designed view that responds to gestures and transitions between subjects, it is also crucial to ensure that the view runs fast and smooth. To avoid a UI that feels slow and sluggish during playback, ensure that animations steadily run at least 60 frames per second.

In order to speed up your view, you might need to eliminate unnecessary code from routines that are frequently used. Start by operating on onDraw(), which will give you the biggest payback. In particular, you should remove allocations in onDraw(), because allocations may result in unnecessary garbage collection that would cause pauses. Allocating objects during initialization, or between animations would also be helpful. In addition, it is considered bad practice to make allocations while you have animation running at the same time.

Another very expensive in terms of resources operation is traversing layouts. Any time a view calls requestLayout(), the Android UI system needs to traverse the entire view hierarchy to find out how big each view has to be. If it finds conflicting measurements, it is going to traverse the hierarchy multiple times. That is why UI designers tend to create deep hierarchies of nested ViewGroup objects to get the UI to behave properly. Yet make sure not to make such view hierarchies too deep as it may cause performance problems.

To summarize, in this chapter, we have discussed the Android Studio UI basics and learned how to interact with its main components and widgets. In particular, we have established how you can manage folders, layouts, strings, and views within the platform. In the next chapter, we shall focus on utilizing the key Android Studio Tools such as the SDK Manager, the AVD Manager, and Navigation Editor.

CHAPTER 4

Android Studio Tools

IN THIS CHAPTER

➤ Going through essential Android Studio Tools

➤ Mastering SDK Manager, AVD Manager, and Navigation Editor

➤ Learning how to generate a Javadoc in Android Studio

In the preceding chapters, you learned how Android Studio can generate code; in this chapter, you will see how Android Studio can refactor your code, its own components, and widgets.

Android development relies on a variety of different tools, whether you decide to go the standard route or opt instead to

DOI: 10.1201/9781003229070-4

apply one of the countless other methods available. In fact, with so many options to get started with, it can sometimes be challenging knowing which is best for you. Which tools are essential? What program do you activate to start coding? This chapter will break down the most popular Android developer tools, including the essential and the optional: Software Development Kit (SDK) Manager, Android Virtual Device (AVD) Manager, and Navigation Editor.

Android SDK here stands for a toolset that enables developers to produce apps for Android OS. It includes the required libraries to build Android apps, a debugger, an emulator, Application Programming Interfaces (APIs), and sample projects with source code, so you can have everything you need for making your own apps.

While there are many different programming languages and a host of Integrated Development Environments (IDEs), the SDK remains a constant. Therefore, we shall start the Android development with the Android SDK.

THE SDK MANAGER

SDK Manager has a wide selection of tools required to build Android apps or to ensure the process goes as smoothly as possible. Whether you end up creating an app with Java, Kotlin or C#, you need the SDK to activate it on an Android device and access unique features of the OS. You will also be able to use an SDK emulator to test apps you have established, monitor your device, and do many other things. Now that the Android SDK comes bundled with Android Studio, the IDE affects the amount of work that gets done and ensures that many of the tools are now accessed and managed.

Even though getting set up with the SDK should be the first Android development lesson you go through, there is still a little more to it than that, and using all of the development tools to their fullest and knowing precisely how the SDK works will definitely result in better apps.

The Android SDK can be installed automatically using the latest version of Gradle or downloading the Android SDK manually in several different ways if that is your preference. Let's take a look at a brief overview of all the different approaches.

Installing the Android SDK (Automated Way)

Latest Gradle 7.0 supports downloading automatically dependencies. Make sure to upgrade to the latest Gradle version otherwise you will see some Gradle plugins that typically manage dependencies to be deprecated in the older versions.

Installing for Ubuntu Linux

In case you are using Ubuntu 15.10 or lower, make sure to install the following standard package. Otherwise, you may get the following notice—"No such file or directory" when trying to execute the apt program that is part of the Android SDK toolset:

```
sudo apt-get install libc6-dev-i386 lib32z1
OpenJDK-8-JDK
```

Installing via Homebrew

In case you have MacOS/OS X running, you can use Homebrew to install the Android SDK. To install

Homebrew – the package manager for MacOS/OS X you need to activate the following commands:

brew tap homebrew/cask

brew install –cask android-SDK

This will install the Android SDK tools in/usr/local/Cellar/android-SDK/<version number>.

Installing the Android SDK (Manual Way)

If you want to install the Android SDK manually, you will need to download the Android SDK without Android Studio bundled. For that, go to Android SDK and navigate to the SDK Tools Only section. Here, copy the URL for the download that is suitable for your build machine.

Next, use wget with the correct SDK URL:

$ wget https://dl.google.com/android/repository/tools_r25.2.3-macosx.zip

After that you need to unzip and place the contents within your home directory. The directory names can be anything you like, but just make sure you save the files somewhere easy to find. In order to run the SDK manager tool insert the following features:

$ tools/bin/sdkmanager –update

$ tools/bin/sdkmanager "platforms;android-25"

"build-tools;25.0.2"   "extras;google;m2repository"
   "cxtras;android;m2repository"

$ tools/bin/sdkmanager –licenses

Afterward, you should set your build environment's PATH variable and other variables that will be applied to locate Android. You might also consider editing your .bash_profile file. And if you are not using bash, you should edit the right config file for your environment. To illustrate:

```
export     ANDROID_SDK_ROOT=/Users/android/
   android-SDK-macosx

export PATH=$PATH:$ANDROID_SDK_ROOT/tools
```

At last, before clicking Save and quitting, reload .bash_ profile one last time:

```
$ source ~/.bash_profile
```

Installing via the GUI

At first, access the prompt, type android, and hit Enter to launch the Android SDK Manager in a window. If this does not work, it means that your PATH variable has not been set up properly with the Android SDK location. It also means that you will need to install the same Android SDK packages on your build machine as you did to get Gradle running locally. Here are the SDK package names you most certainly need to start with:

Tools > Android SDK Tools

Tools > Android SDK Platform-tools

Tools > Android SDK Build-tools

In addition, you will also want to download some extras:

Android Support Repository

Android Support Library

After that, choose the Android SDK Build-tools for the version of Android that you listed in the build.Gradle file as the android: buildToolsVersion target. If your build.gradle says

```
android {
    buildToolsVersion "21"
        . . .
}
```

then make sure to download that API version in the Android SDK Manager.

Installing via the Command Line

It is also possible to download the SDK packages using the following command line with the –no-ui parameter:

android update SDK –no-ui –all

In case you want to be selective about installing, you can use android list to view all the packages and apply the –filter option for selective installs in such a manner:

sudo android update SDK –no-UI –filter platform-tools, tools

And once you decide to be selective about which packages to be installed, you also need to make sure to include the following extra Android Maven repository. Otherwise, you may not be able to use the latest support design library:

android update SDK –no-ui –all –filter extra-android-m2repository

Anatomy of the Android SDK

The Android SDK can be broken down into several main components. These include:

- Platform-tools
- Build-tools
- SDK-tools
- The Android Debug Bridge (ADB)
- Android Emulator

Surely the most important parts of this package are in the SDK tools. You will require these tools regardless of which version of Android you are targeting. These are what actually constitute the Android Package Kit (APK)—turning your Java program into an Android app that can be operated even on a phone. These include a number of build tools, debugging tools, and image tools. A great example of such a tool is the Dalvik Debug Monitor Server (DDMS) debugging service, which is what lets us use the Android Device Monitor to check the status of an Android device.

The Build tools were previously categorized under the same heading as the Platform-tools but have since been decoupled in later versions so that they can be updated separately. As the name suggests, these are also crucially important to build your Android apps. An example of such tools could be the Zipalign tool, which optimizes the app to request minimal memory when running prior to generating the final APK, and the Apksigner that signs the APK for consequent verification.

The Platform-tools could be more specifically adjusted to the version of Android that you need to target. Typically, it is considered best to install the latest Platform-tools, which are normally installed by default. However, after the first installation, you need to keep your Platform-tools constantly updated. The tools are backward compatible, meaning that they are used to support older versions of Android too.

To summarize, many of the above-mentioned tools are key for SDK testing, debugging, and packaging. They provide a kind of link between Android Studio and a physical device or emulator so that your app can be specifically packaged and then tested as you go. It is safe to leave the SDK alone for the most development part: Android Studio will recommend necessary updates, and it will call upon the required elements when you click Run or Build APK.

That said, a few of the tools are also directly accessible, which will be applied for operations like updating the SDK, or directly monitoring and modifying your Android device. While Android Studio will normally let you know when you have to update something, you can also manage updates to the SDK manually via the manager. You can find this in Android Studio if you navigate to Tools—Android—SDK Manager. Activating the Manage will let you do things like choosing the size of the device and other specifications, and you will be prompted to download the requisite ×86 system image if it is not already installed.

Using the ADB

Using ADB is a little different. It is a program that allows you to communicate with any Android device. In its foundation, it relies on Platform-tools in order to read through the Android version that is being used on said device, and hence it is included in the Platform-tools package. You can use ADB to access shell tools such as Logcat, review your device ID, or even install apps.

To access ADB, you will need to find your Android SDK installation folder and navigate to the platform-tools directory. On Windows, hold shift and right-click anywhere in the folder to open a command line. On Mac, just open Terminal from Launchpad that is located in the Other folder).

ADB is a flexible command-line tool that allows you to interact with a device. The ADB command can manage a variety of device actions, such as installing and debugging apps, and it provides access to a Unix shell that you can administer to run a variety of commands on a device. For example, if you type "adb devices," you will get a list of the Android devices that are plugged in, along with their Device

IDs. And if you script "adb install [options] package-name" you will be authorized to remotely install an APK.

It is also considered to be a client-server program that includes the following three components:

1. A client, which forwards commands. The client runs on your development machine, and you can invoke a client from a command-line terminal by issuing one of the ADB commands.

2. A daemon (adbd), which runs commands on a device. The daemon typically runs as a background process on each device.

3. A server, which establishes communication between the client and the daemon. The server runs as a background process on your development machine.

As already mentioned, ADB is included in the Android SDK Platform-Tools package. You can download this package with the SDK Manager, which installs it at android_sdk/platform-tools/. When you first launch an ADB client, the client checks whether an ADB server is already running. Only if there is not, it starts the server process. When the server starts, it links to local TCP port 5037 and registers all commands sent from adb clients – all adb clients use port 5037 to communicate with the ADB server.

The server then establishes connections to all running devices. It locates emulators by scanning odd-numbered ports in the range 5555–5585, the range used by the first 16 emulators. Where the server finds an ADB daemon (adbd), it sets up a connection to that port. Each emulator uses a pair of sequential ports – an even-numbered port for console connections and an odd-numbered port for ADB connections. For example:

- Emulator 1, console: 5555
- Emulator 1, adb: 5556
- Emulator 2, console: 5557
- Emulator 2, adb: 5558

As shown, the emulator connected to adb on port 5554 is the same as the emulator whose console listens on port 5556.

Once the server completed establishing connections to all devices, you can use ADB commands to access those devices. Because the server manages connections to devices as well as commands from multiple adb clients, you can also control any device from any client or a script.

In order to use adb with a device connected over USB, you should enable USB debugging in the device system settings, under Developer options. On Android 4.2 and higher, the Developer options screen is hidden by default. To make it visible, go to Settings > About phone and tap Build number seven times. When you return to the previous screen, you will be able to find Developer options at the bottom. You can now connect your device with USB. Verify that your device is connected by implementing adb devices from the android_sdk/platform-tools/directory. Once connected, you will be able to see the device name listed as a "device."

The Android Emulator

The Android Emulator simulates Android devices on your computer so that you can test your application on a variety of devices and Android API levels without having to interact with each physical device.

The emulator can imitate almost all of the capabilities of a real Android device. Thus, you can reproduce incoming phone calls and text messages, specify the location of the device, simulate different network speeds, simulate rotation and hardware sensors, as well as access the Google Play Store.

Test-running your app on the emulator is definitely faster and easier than doing so on a physical device. For instance, you can transfer data faster to the emulator than to a device connected over USB. It is also convenient that the emulator comes with predefined configurations for various Android phones, tablets, Wear OS, and Android TV devices.

Each instance of the Android Emulator uses an AVD to specify the simulated device's Android version and hardware functions. To productively test your app, you should create an AVD that reproduces each device on which your app is prescribed to run. In order to create and manage AVDs, you can use the AVD Manager.

Each AVD operates as an independent device, with its own private storage for user data and Secure Digital card. By default, the emulator stores the user data, SD card data, and cache in a directory specific to that AVD. So that when you launch the emulator, it loads the user data and SD card data from the AVD directory.

Running an App on the Android Emulator   You can run an app from an Android Studio project, or you could run an app that has been installed on the Android Emulator as you would run any app on a device. In order to start the Android Emulator and run an app in your project:

In Android Studio, create an AVD that the emulator can use to install and run your app. In the toolbar, select the AVD that you need to run your app on from the target device drop-down menu and click Run.

In case you see an error or warning message at the top of the dialog, click the link to correct the problem or to get more information. Certain errors such as Hardware Accelerated Execution Manager (Intel HAXM) errors you should fix before you can continue.

For MacOS, if you see the following Warning: No DNS servers found error when starting the emulator, check to see whether you have an /etc/resolv.conf file. If you do not have this file, enter the following command in a terminal window:

ln -s /private/var/run/resolv.conf /etc/resolv.conf

It is currently impossible to use the emulator's extended controls when it's running in a tool window. If your development workflow relies heavily on the extended controls, continue to use the Android Emulator as a standalone application. Additionally, certain virtual devices – such as Android TV and foldable devices – cannot be executed in Android Studio because they have specific UI requirements or important functions in the extended controls.

Navigate the Emulator Screen   In order to navigate the emulator screen, you can use your computer mouse pointer to mimic your finger on the touchscreen. Moreover, you can type characters and enter the following emulator shortcuts presented in Table 4.1.[1]

---

[1] https://developer.android.com/studio/run/emulator?hl=fr, Android

TABLE 4.1   Emulator Shortcuts

Feature	Description
Swipe the screen	Point to the screen, press and hold the primary mouse button, swipe across the screen, and then release.
Drag an item	Point to an item on the screen, press and hold the primary mouse button, move the item, and then release.
Tap (touch)	Point to the screen, press the primary mouse button and then release. For example, you could click a text field to start typing in it, select an app, or press a button.
Double-tap	Point to the screen, press the primary mouse button quickly twice and then release.
Touch and hold	Point to an item on the screen, press the primary mouse button, hold, and then release. For example, you could open options for an item.
Type	You can type in the emulator by using your computer keyboard, or using a keyboard that pops up on the emulator screen. For example, you could type in a text field after you selected it.
Pinch and spread	Pressing Control (Command on Mac) brings up a pinch gesture multi-touch interface. The mouse acts as the first finger, and across the anchor point is the second finger. Drag the cursor to move the first point. Clicking the left mouse button acts like touching down both points, and releasing acts like picking both up.
Vertical swipe	Open a vertical menu on the screen and use the scroll wheel (mouse wheel) to scroll through the menu items until you see the one you want. Click the menu item to select it.

Install and Add Files

In order to install an APK file on the emulated device, simply move an APK file onto the emulator screen. An APK Installer dialog shall appear and when the installation completes, you will be able to see the app in your apps list.

To add a file to the emulated device, just drag the file onto the emulator screen. The file is located in the/sdcard/ Download/directory. You can view the file from Android Studio using the Device File Explorer, or look for it from the device using the Downloads or Files app, depending on the device version.

Snapshots

A snapshot is a stored image of an AVD that saves the entire layout of the device at the time that it was saved – including OS settings, application state, and user data. You can address to a saved system state by loading a snapshot anytime you want, saving you the time of waiting for the operating system and applications on the virtual device to restart, as well as saving you the resources of bringing your app back to the state at which you want to continue your testing. Starting a virtual device should be viewed as waking a physical device from a sleep mode, as opposed to knocking it from a powered-off state.

For each AVD, you can have one Quick Boot snapshot and any number of general snapshots. The easiest way to take advantage of snapshots is to use Quick Boot snapshots: By default, each AVD is set to automatically take a Quick Boot snapshot on exit and load from a Quick Boot snapshot on start.

The first time that an AVD starts, it should activate a cold boot, just like powering on a device. If Quick Boot is enabled, all subsequent starts load from the specified snapshot, and the system is restored to the state scripted in that snapshot.

Snapshots are valid for the system image, AVD configuration, and emulator features with which they are saved. In case you make a change in any of these domains, all snapshots of the modified AVD become invalid. Similarly, any update to the Android Emulator, system image, or AVD settings resets the AVD's saved state, so the next time you start the AVD, it would perform a cold boot.

Using the SDK Independently

In case you are determined to explore the SDK independently, you can find a whole subdirectory within the SDK folder called "Docs" and this will give you access to some useful information. For the most part, though, it is recommended to visit https://developer.android.com/ instead.

Previously the Android SDK would come packaged with a selection of useful sample projects. Yet nowadays this is no longer the case, but it is still possible to find them instead by opening Android Studio and navigating to File – New – Import Sample.

Although the Android SDK and Android Studio are closely linked, you will not always want to use them together. You may need to use another IDE, for example, if you want to streamline the process of making a 3D game (in which case, you may wish to use Unity or Unreal solutions as well), or in case you are interested in cross-platform mobile development (in which case you might apply Xamarin).

In any case, you will need to show the chosen IDE where the SDK is located, usually by scripting the path somewhere. You can also find the location of the Android SDK in Android Studio, in case you might ever need to move it, or just use it for your own reference. Just go to File – Project Structure. Here you will also be able to see the location of the JDK as well as the Android Native Development Kit (NDK).

You can choose the location of the SDK when you are going through the installation. If you left this option as default though, then there might be a chance it may be in the AppData\Local directory. Be aware that this folder is hidden on Windows by default, so it might take some time to find it.

The previously mentioned NDK allows you to build apps using native languages like C and C++. With these, you can access certain libraries and boost more performance out of a device – making it applicable for game development, among other things.

As mentioned, if it is just the SDK you are interested in, then you can download this on its own by visiting the downloads page and then choosing to include the SDK manager. This will allow you to update the SDK through the command line. There are also ways to access the AVD Manager without Android Studio. But for the vast majority of users, it is much simpler to just install the full suite and enjoy the graphical interface and other functionalities – even if they intend on using a different IDE for development.

THE AVD MANAGER

An AVD is a configuration that defines the characteristics of an Android phone, tablet, Wear OS, Android TV, or Automotive OS device that you are going to simulate in the Android Emulator. The AVD Manager, therefore, is an interface you can launch from Android Studio that helps you create and operate AVDs.

To open the AVD Manager, proceed to the Select Tools function and Click on the AVD Manager option in the toolbar.

An AVD contains a hardware profile, system image, storage area, skin, and other attributes. Generally, it is recommended to create an AVD for each system image that your app could potentially support based on the <uses-sdk> setting in your manifest.

The hardware profile sets the characteristics of a device as shipped from the factory. The AVD Manager comes preloaded with certain hardware profiles, such as Pixel devices, but you can also customize the hardware profiles as needed. However, not all hardware profiles are indicated to include Play Store. Meaning that only some profiles are fully compliant with the Compatibility Test Suite (CTS) and may use system images that include the Play Store app.

System Images

A system image labeled with Google APIs normally includes access to Google Play services. A system image labeled with the Google Play logo in the Play Store column includes the Google Play Store app and access to Google Play services, including a Google Play tab in the Extended controls dialog that provides a convenient button for updating Google Play services on the device.

To ensure app security and smooth experience with physical devices, system images with the Google Play Store included are signed with a release key, which means that you will not be able to get elevated privileges (root) with these images. Suppose you require elevated privileges (root) to help with your app troubleshooting. In that case, you can use the Android Open Source Project (AOSP) system images that do not include Google apps or services.

Storage Area

The AVD also has an additional storage area on your development machine. It is mostly used to store the device user data, such as installed apps and settings, as well as an emulated SD card. If required, you can use the AVD Manager to wipe user data, so the device has the same data as if it were new.

Skin

To put it simply, an emulator skin is responsible for the appearance of a device. The AVD Manager has some predefined skins you can choose from. Additionally, you can also define your own, or use skins specified by third parties.

Creating an AVD

To create a new AVD, open the AVD Manager by clicking Tools > AVD Manager. Then choose Create Virtual Device, at the bottom of the AVD Manager dialog. At the Select

Hardware page choose a hardware profile, and then click Next. If you don't see the hardware profile you want, you can create or import a hardware profile. Once the System Image page appears, select the system image for a particular API level, and then click Next. If you see Download next to the system image, you need to click it to download the system image. You must be connected to the internet to download it.

The API level of the target device is important, because your app will not be able to run on a system image with an API level that is less than that required by your app, as specified in the minSdkVersion attribute of the app manifest file.

If your app declares a <uses-library> element in the manifest file, the app requires a system image in which that external library is present. In case you need to run your app on an emulator, create an AVD that includes the required library. To do so, you might need to use an add-on component for the AVD platform; for example, the Google APIs add-on that contains the Google Maps library.

On the next Verify Configuration page that appears change AVD properties as needed, and then click Finish. Click Show Advanced Settings to show more settings, such as the skin.

The new AVD should be displayed in the Your Virtual Devices page or the Select Deployment Target dialog. In addition, it is possible to create an AVD starting with a copy: From the Your Virtual Devices page of the AVD Manager, right-click an AVD and select Duplicate. After that, on the Verify Configuration page that appears, click Change or Previous if you need to make changes on the System Image and Select Hardware pages. Make your changes, and then click Finish. The AVD will be presented on the Your Virtual Devices page.

Creating a Hardware Profile

The AVD Manager offers redefined hardware profiles for common devices so you can easily add them to your AVD definitions. In case you need to define a different device, you can make a new hardware profile. You have an option of defining a new hardware profile from the beginning or copying a hardware profile as a start. However, keep in mind that preloaded hardware profiles are not editable.

In order to create a new hardware profile from the beginning, go to the Select Hardware page and access New Hardware Profile. In the Configure Hardware Profile page, change the hardware profile properties as needed and then just click Finish.

Your new hardware profile would then appear on the Select Hardware page. You can also create an AVD that uses the hardware profile by clicking Next. Or, alternatively, click Cancel to return to the Your Virtual Devices page or Select Deployment Target dialog.

In case you want to create a hardware profile starting with a copy you would have to go to the same Select Hardware page, select a hardware profile and click Clone Device. After that, you can change the hardware profile properties as you might require in the Configure Hardware Profile page. Once you are done, do not forget to click Finish.

Your new hardware profile would then appear on the Select Hardware page. You can additionally create an AVD that uses the hardware profile by clicking Next. Or return to the Your Virtual Devices page or Select Deployment Target dialog by simply clicking Cancel.

There are certain operations you can perform on an existing AVD from the Your Virtual Devices page:

1. To edit an AVD, click Edit this AVD and save your changes.

2. To delete an AVD, right-click an AVD and select Delete. Or click Menu and select Delete.

3. To show the associated AVD .ini and .img files on disk, right-click an AVD and select Show on Disk. Or click Menu and select Show on Disk.

4. To review AVD configuration data, you can include in any bug reports to the Android Studio team, right-click an AVD and select View Details. Or click Menu and select View Details.

If you are looking to edit existing hardware profiles, from the same Select Hardware page, you can perform the following operations:

1. To edit a hardware profile, select it and click Edit Device. Or right-click a hardware profile and select Edit. After that, make your changes.

2. To delete a hardware profile, right-click it and select Delete.

3. Make sure to note that you cannot edit or delete the predefined hardware profiles.

When it comes to AVD properties, you can specify the following properties in Table 4.2 for AVD configurations

TABLE 4.2 AVD Properties List[2]

AVD Property	Description
AVD name	Name of the AVD. The name can contain uppercase or lowercase letters, numbers from 0 to 9, periods (.), underscores (_), parentheses (()), dashes (−), and spaces. The name of the file storing the AVD configuration is derived from the AVD name.
AVD ID (advanced)	The AVD filename is derived from the ID, and you can use the ID to refer to the AVD from the command line.
Hardware profile	Click Change to select a different hardware profile on the Select Hardware page.
System image	Click Change to select a different system image on the System Image page. An active internet connection is required to download a new image.
Startup orientation	Select one option for the initial emulator orientation: • Portrait – Oriented taller than wide. • Landscape – Oriented wider than tall. An option is enabled only if it is selected in the hardware profile. When running the AVD in the emulator, you can change the orientation if both portrait and landscape are supported in the hardware profile.

[2] https://developer.android.com/studio/run/managing-avds?hl=fr, Android

(Continued)

TABLE 4.2 (Continued)   AVD Properties List

AVD Property	Description
Camera (advanced)	To enable a camera, select one or both options: • Front – The lens faces away from the user. • Back – The lens faces toward the user. The Emulated setting produces a software-generated image, while the Webcam setting uses your development computer webcam to take a picture. This option is available only if it is selected in the hardware profile.
Network: speed (advanced)	Select a network protocol to determine the speed of data transfer: • GSM – Global System for Mobile Communications • HSCSD – High-Speed Circuit-Switched Data • GPRS – Generic Packet Radio Service • EDGE – Enhanced Data rates for GSM Evolution • UMTS – Universal Mobile Telecommunications System • HSDPA – High-Speed Downlink Packet Access • LTE – Long-Term Evolution • Full (default) – Transfer data as quickly as your computer allows
Network: latency (advanced)	Select a network protocol to set how much time (delay) it takes for the protocol to transfer a data packet from one point to another point.

(Continued)

TABLE 4.2 (Continued) AVD Properties List

AVD Property	Description
Emulated performance: graphics	Select how graphics are rendered in the emulator: • Hardware – Use your computer graphics card for faster rendering. • Software – Emulate the graphics in software, which is useful if you're having a problem with rendering in your graphics card. • Automatic – Let the emulator decide the best option based on your graphics card.
Emulated performance: boot option (advanced)	• Cold boot – Start the device each time by powering up from the device-off state. • Quick boot – Start the device by loading the device state from a saved snapshot.
Emulated performance: multi-core CPU (advanced)	Select the number of processor cores on your computer that you would like to use for the emulator. Using more processor cores speeds up the emulator.
Memory and storage: RAM	The amount of RAM on the device. This value is set by the hardware manufacturer, but you can override it, if needed, such as for faster emulator operation. Increasing the size uses more resources on your computer. Type a RAM size and select the units, one of B (byte), KB (kilobyte), MB (megabyte), GB (gigabyte), or TB (terabyte).
Memory and storage: VM heap	The VM heap size. This value is set by the hardware manufacturer, but you can override it if needed. Type a heap size and select the units, one of B (byte), KB (kilobyte), MB (megabyte), GB (gigabyte), or TB (terabyte).

(Continued)

TABLE 4.2 (Continued)   AVD Properties List

AVD Property	Description
Memory and storage: internal storage	The amount of nonremovable memory space available on the device. The hardware manufacturer sets this value, but you can override it if needed. Type size and select the units, one of B (byte), KB (kilobyte), MB (megabyte), GB (gigabyte), or TB (terabyte).
Memory and storage: SD card	The amount of removable memory space available to store data on the device. To use a virtual SD card managed by Android Studio, select Studio-managed, type size, and select the units, one of B (byte), KB (kilobyte), MB (megabyte), GB (gigabyte), or TB (terabyte). A minimum of 100 MB is recommended to use the camera. To manage the space in a file, select External file and click Specify the file and location.
Device frame: enable device frame	Select to enable a frame around the emulator window that mimics the look of a real device.
Custom skin definition (advanced)	Select a skin that controls what the device looks like when displayed in the emulator. Remember that specifying a screen size that is too big for the skin can mean that the screen is cut off, so you cannot see the whole screen.
Keyboard: enable keyboard input (advanced)	Select this option if you want to use your hardware keyboard to interact with the emulator.

in the Verify Configuration page. The AVD configuration identifies the interaction between the development computer and the emulator and properties you need to override in the hardware profile.

Typically, AVD configuration properties override hardware profile properties. Yet emulator properties that you set while the emulator is running can override them both.

THE NAVIGATION EDITOR

Navigation between different screens and apps is the main part of the user experience. The following principles set a foundation for a stable yet intuitive user experience across apps. The Navigation component is designed to execute these principles by default, making sure that users can apply the same techniques and patterns in navigation as they move between apps.

It is also great at simplifying navigation implementation through the library, while also helping you visualize your app's navigation flow. The library has a number of benefits that include:

- Automatic handling of fragment transactions

- Correctly handling up to and back by default

- Default behaviors for animations and transitions

- Deep linking as a first-class operation

- Implementing navigation UI patterns (navigation drawers and bottom nav) with little additional work

- Ensure safety when passing information while navigating

- Android Studio tooling for visualizing and modifying the navigation flow of an app

Navigation could also be perceived as a framework for navigating between "destinations" within an Android application that provides a consistent API whether destinations are treated as fragments, activities, or other items.

Normally, the Navigation component consists of three key parts:

1. **Navigation graph (New XML resource):** This is a resource that holds all navigation-related information in one centralized location. This includes all the places in your app, known as destinations, and possible paths a user could follow through your app.

2. **NavHostFragment (Layout XML view):** This is a special widget you include in your layout. It displays different destinations from your navigation graph.

3. **NavController (Kotlin/Java object):** This is a subject that keeps track of the current position within the navigation graph. It administers swapping destination content in the NavHostFragment as you move through a navigation graph.

The navigation editor is a standard part of Android Studio 3.3 and higher. Therefore, in case you are still using Android Studio 3.2, navigation would be an experimental feature for you and you will have to manually enable it:

In your file, go to Settings and select the Experimental category. Here you just need to click on the Enable Navigation option.

Gradle Plugins

Before you can create your own navigation graph, you need to take care of certain item dependencies. Thus, you should add the following dependencies for the artifacts you are going to use in the build.Gradle file for your app or module:[3]

```
dependencies {

    - def nav_version = "2.1.0-beta01"

    - def nav_version_ktx = "2.1.0-beta01"
```

---

[3] https://medium.com/@muhamed.riyas/navigation-component-the-complete-guide-c51c9911684, Medium

//For Java

- implementation "androidx.navigation:navigation-fragment:$nav_version"

- implementation "androidx.navigation:navigation-ui:$nav_version"

//For Kotlin

- implementation "androidx.navigation:navigation-fragment-ktx:$nav_version_ktx"

- implementation "androidx.navigation:navigation-ui-ktx:$nav_version_ktx"

Additionally, you have to apply the following plugins in the build.gradle of your app module:

- apply plugin: "com.android.application"

- apply plugin: "kotlin-android"

- apply plugin: "kotlin-android-extensions"

- apply plugin: "androidx.navigation.safeargs.kotlin"

- You must have android.useAndroidX=true in your gradle.properties file as per Migrating to AndroidX – android.useAndroidX=true

After all the plugins are configured, you can start creating Navigation component for your application with a single activity and couple of fragments.

Following are major Navigation components that you should be familiar with:

- Your MainActivity class
- A couple of fragments
- Navigation graph
- Action
- Destinations
- Pop Up To
- Arguments
- Deep linking
- Navigation Host Fragment
- Navigation Controller

The first two items on the list are generic to most other functionalities that we have discussed previously. Therefore, it is suggested to focus on fragments typical to the creation of the Navigation component, which will help you to relate things with what you know and avoid any confusion.

Navigation Graph

A navigation graph is a resource file that keeps all of your destinations and actions. The graph is used to display all of your app's navigation paths.

Standard navigation usually consists of destinations represented by a preview thumbnail, and connecting actions that are represented by arrows that show how users can navigate from one destination to another.

Destinations could also be perceived as different content areas of your app. And actions are logical connections between your destinations that represent paths that users can take.

Creating a navigation graph is a pretty straightforward process with several simple steps to go through.

1. Create a navigation resource file "app_navigation. xml". The name could be anything you assign to it, yet it has to follow the basic resource file name rules (for instance, contain only lowercase a–z, 0–9, or underscore).

   So after creating the "app_navigation.xml" your code should look like this:

```
<?xml version="1.0" encoding="utf-8"?>
<navigation xmlns:android="http://
schemas.android.com/apk/res/android"
 xmlns:app="http://schemas.android.
com/apk/res-auto"
 xmlns:tools="http://schemas.android.
com/tools"
 android:id="@+id/app_navigation"
 >
</navigation>
```

2. The next steps should be defining the first navigation view that is from where the navigation should start and to where the navigation should navigate. Such details are commanding through tag called "destination." In addition, you can also use the following three fragments to describe the concept of the destination you work at the time:

- MyHomeFragment

- MySecondFragment

- MyThirdFragment

3. Once you are done with the defining step, you should Add all the fragments as child elements into the navigation parent, making sure that you are assigned some unique id to your fragments. To illustrate with an example:[4]

```
<?xml version="1.0" encoding="utf-8"?>
<navigation xmlns:android="http://
schemas.android.com/apk/res/android"
xmlns:app="http://schemas.android.com/
apk/res-auto"
xmlns:tools="http://schemas.android.
com/tools"
android:id="@+id/app_navigation">
    <fragment
        android:id="@+id/
myHomeFragment"
      android:name="com.navigation.
component.sample.ui.fragments.
MyHomeFragment"
              android:label=
"fragment_my_home"
            tools:layout="@layout/
fragment_my_home">
    </fragment>
```

[4] https://medium.com/@muhamed.riyas/navigation-component-the-complete-guide-c51c9911684, Medium

```
    <fragment android:id="@+id/
mySecondFragment"
                android:name="com.
navigation.component.sample.
ui.fragments.MySecondFragment"

android:label="fragment_my_second"
                tools:layout="@layout/
fragment_my_second">
    </fragment>
    <fragment android:id="@+id/
myThirdFragment"
                android:name="com.
navigation.component.sample.
ui.fragments.MyThirdFragment"

android:label="fragment_my_third"
                tools:layout="@layout/
fragment_my_third">
            </fragment>
</navigation>
```

You should have noticed that the following four key parameters were added to highlight certain id features to your code:

1. **android:id:** Unique id for the fragment, just like we are assigning id to any other widgets in XML layout.

2. **android:name:** It is the fully qualified name of your fragment class in kotlin/java.

3. **android:label:** A string to identify the fragment.

4. **tools:layout:** An id of layout resource file from res/ layout.

Action

As already stated, the navigation system also lets you navigate via actions. In order to add action in a fragment we can use tag inside the tag. At the same time, it is possible to define more than one action with a different id.

There are certain parameters used inside :

- **android:id:** Unique id for the action, just like we are assigned id to the fragments.

- **app:destination:** The unique id of the destination fragment, means this action will move the current view to the destination fragment.

- **app:popUpTo:** This is for backward navigation if the app has navigated from a fragment A to fragment B, then fragment B to fragment C. If you want to go fragment A to fragment C you can use this parameter value as the id fragment A. The Navigation component will operate the back stack management and the lifecycle.

Also, if you want to include the animations for the fragment transaction as specified, you should simply create the XML animation file inside res/anim folder. With that, you are now ready with navigation design and can go ahead with navigation calls using NavHostFragment and NavigationController.

NavHostFragment

In order to modify your Navigations activity layouts, it has to contain a special widget called a NavHostFragment. A NavHostFragment interchanges different fragment destinations in and out as you go through the navigation graph. To illustrate with an example:

```
LinearLayout
    .../>
    <androidx.appcompat.widget.Toolbar
        .../>
    <fragment
        android:layout_width=
"match_parent"
        android:layout_height="0dp"
        android:layout_weight="1"
        android:id="@+id/
my_nav_host_fragment"
        android:name="androidx.navigation.
fragment.NavHostFragment"
        app:navGraph="@navigation/
app_navigation"
        app:defaultNavHost="true"
        />
    <com.google.android.material.
bottomnavigation.BottomNavigationView
```

This is considered to be a feature for the standard activity that contains global navigation, including a bottom nav and a toolbar.

Here, the android:name="androidx.navigation.fragment.NavHostFragment" and app:defaultNavHost="true" connect the system back button to the NavHostFragment app:navGraph="@navigation/app_navigation" and also associate the NavHostFragment with a navigation graph. This navigation graph specifies all the destinations the user can navigate to, in this NavHostFragment.

NavigationController

NavController is very convenient because when you call methods like navigate() or popBackStack(), it translates these commands into the appropriate framework operations based on the type of destination you are navigating to or from. For instance, when you call navigate() with an activity destination, the NavController calls startActivity() on your behalf.

There are few ways to insert NavigationController:

- Fragment.findNavController()

- View.findNavController()

- Activity.findNavController(viewId: Int)

When navigating to a Destination with NavController you will first have to link up the Navigate To Destination button to navigate to the mySecondFragment destination (which is a destination that is a MySecondFragment. And then open MyHomeFragment.kt or your java fragment file and activate the onClick listener or any other user action and finally navigate as follows:

```
view?.findViewById<Button>(R.id.button)
.setOnClickListener(View.OnClickListener {
```

```
findNavController().navigate(R.
id.action_myHomeFragment_to_
mySecondFragment)
```

SafeArgs

SafeArgs is another Navigation component that has a Gradle plugin and generates simple object and builder classes for type-safe access to arguments specified for destinations and actions. For example, since we previously used the <argument> tag for MySecondFragment, SafeArgs will produce a class called MySecondFragmentArgs.

At the same time, SafeArgs have different parcelable classes for arguments as well as various data types. Below is the complete table of SafeArgs data types supported by android (Table 4.3).

GENERATING A JAVADOC

In this last section, we shall discuss Javadoc, a helpful tool for generating documentation directly from your Java source files. This little part dedicated to Javadoc is only going to cover the basic background, although it is hoped that developers-to-be shall look for more resources and tutorials for learning Java in order to create more sophisticated Android applications.

Javadoc could also be viewed as a utility provided with the Java SDK that allows specialists to generate code documentation from Java source files. Development environments like Eclipse have built-in support for Javadoc and can generate searchable HTML reference data from Javadoc-style comments. In fact, the Android SDK reference is basically a form of Javadoc documentation.

TABLE 4.3 SafeArgs Data Types Supported by the Android Navigation Library[5]

Type	app:argType Syntax	Supports Default Values?	Supports Null Values?
Integer	app:argType="integer"	Yes	No
Float	app:argType="float"	Yes	No
Long	app:argType="long"	Yes - Default values must always end with an "L" suffix (e.g. "123L").	No
Boolean	app:argType="boolean"	Yes – "true" or "false"	No
String	app:argType="string"	Yes	Yes
Resource reference	app:argType="reference"	Yes – Default values must be in the form of "@resourceType/resourceName" (e.g. "@style/myCustomStyle") or "0"	No
Custom parcelable	app:argType="<type>", where <type> is the fully-qualified class name of the Parcelable	Supports a default value of "@null." Does not support other default values.	Yes
Custom serializable	app:argType="<type>", where <type> is the fully-qualified class name of the Serializable	Supports a default value of "@null." Does not support other default values.	Yes
Custom enum	app:argType="<type>", where <type> is the fully-qualified name of the enum	Yes – Default values must match the unqualified name.	No

[5] https://developer.android.com/guide/navigation/navigation-pass-data#supported_argument_types, Android

Javadoc documentation uses a combination of processing the source code and inspecting types and parameters while reading special comment tags that the developer provides as metadata related to a section of code.

Normally, a Javadoc-style comment should be coming just before the code it is associated with. For example, a Javadoc comment for a class should be just above the class declaration and comment for a method should be just above the method declaration. Additionally, each comment should begin with a short description, followed by an option longer description. Then you can include a number of different metadata tags, which should be supplied in a specific order. Some important tags include:

@author – who wrote this code

@version – when was it changed

@param – describe method parameters

@return – describe method return values

@throws – describe exceptions thrown

@see – link to other, related items

@since – describe when code was introduced

@deprecated – describe a deprecated item and what alternative to use instead

At the same time, keep in mind that it is possible for you to create your own custom tags for use in documentation.

As mentioned, the Javadoc documentation is formed mainly of comments that are usually placed above classes, methods, or fields. Therefore, it is important to learn how to manipulate and modify comment components first.

Adding a New Comment

You can add a Javadoc simply by using automatic comments completion that is enabled by default. You should type/** before a declaration and press Enter, the IDE will auto-complete the rest of the doc comment for you.

Add a Javadoc Using Context Actions

You may also add a Javadoc through context actions by placing the caret at the declaration in the editor and selecting Add Javadoc from the list. Moreover, there is also an additional option for method comments, as the new comment stub contains the required tags (@param tags for each method parameter, @return, or @throws). At the same time, in Kotlin, the @param and other tags are not generated because the recommended style requires incorporating the description of parameters and return values directly into the documentation comment.

Disable Automatic Comments

In order to disable automatic comments, go to the Settings/Preferences dialog, select Editor's Smart Keys option, and clear the Insert documentation comment stub checkbox.

Fix a Javadoc

In case a method signature has been changed, IDE will highlight the tag that does not match the method signature and suggest a quick fix. If you agree with it, just press Alt+Enter to apply that fix.

You can also update an existing Javadoc comment in order to account for the changes in the declaration using the Fix doc comment action. For that, place the caret within a class, method, function, or field, and press Ctrl+Shift+A. Type fix doc comment and press Enter. Furthermore, you can use the Fix doc comment action to add missing documentation stub with the corresponding tags: Place the caret within a class, method, or function and invoke the action.

Render Javadocs

The android platform allows you to render Javadocs in the editor. Typically, rendered comments are easier to read, and they do not overload your code with extra tags.

In order to adjust the rendered view, you need to click Toggle rendered view in the gutter next to the necessary documentation comment (or press Ctrl+Alt+Q). Then click Artwork Edit feature to modify the comment.

Rendered Javadocs also let you click links to go to the referenced web pages, or view quick documentation for the referenced topics. If you want to change the font size, right-click a Javadoc in the editor and select Adjust Font Size from the context menu. Keep in mind that the rendered comments use the same font size as the quick documentation popup.

Render Javadocs by Default

You can also set the IDE to always render Javadocs in the editor. For that, simply right-click the icon in the gutter and select Enable the Render All option.

Alternatively, in the Settings/Preferences dialog Ctrl+Alt+S, select Appearance feature and enable the Render documentation comments option. In case you want to edit rendered Javadocs, you can click the Toggle Rendered View icon in the gutter next to the comment.

Generate a Javadoc Reference

Android Studio provides a great utility that enables you to generate a Javadoc reference for your project. From the main menu, select Tools and Generate JavaDoc option. In the dialog that opens, select a scope of files or directories for which you want to generate the reference, and set the output directory where you want generated documentation to be placed.

The Output directory is an obligatory field: you cannot generate a Javadoc file as long it is empty.

Instead, use the slider to determine the visibility level of components that will be included in the generated documentation. You can select one of the following options:

- **Private:** to include all classes and members to the reference

- **Package:** to include all classes and members except the private ones

- **Protected:** to include public and protected classes and members

- **Public:** to include only public classes and members

Once that is set, it is also advised to specify a locale (for example en_US.UTF-8), command-line arguments, and the maximum heap size. When finished, click OK to generate the reference.

View Javadocs in the Editor

On the platform, you can view Javadocs for any symbol or method signature right from the editor. To enable such a function, you should configure library documentation paths or add downloaded Javadocs to the IDE.

Just move the mouse to the necessary symbol to view its documentation, or place the caret at the symbol, and press Ctrl+Q to be able to view documentation, and switch between the popup and the toolbar. Next, click the Show Options Menu icon in the popup to change the font size, display the quick documentation toolbar, or go to the source code.

Troubleshoot

Typically, the most widely known Javadoc error that appears is Malformed locale name: en_US.UTF-8.

Thankfully, there is a pretty simple solution that one should remember at all times. Start by clearing the Locale field and once that is done, add -encoding utf8 -docencoding utf8 -charset utf8 functions in the Other command-line arguments field.

Here, -encoding segment will specify the encoding of the source files. The – docencoding part shall identify the encoding of the output HTML files while -charset stands for the charset specified in the HTML head section of the output files. Once you have completed this insertion, just reload the file to see if the error has been settled.

To summarize this chapter, we described the most popular Android developer tools and proceeded to implement some of their features. We defined the essential and the optional instruments such as the SDK Manager, the AVD Manager, and Navigation Editor. We introduced the required libraries to build Android apps, a debugger, an emulator, APIs, and sample projects with source code. The next chapter will complete the Android Studio toolset by learning about Android Device Monitor and Debugging procedures. We shall also review some of the most useful shortcuts and button techniques that one might need.

CHAPTER 5

Debugging

IN THIS CHAPTER

- ➤ Learning about the main Running and Debugging processes

- ➤ Handling Android Device Monitor Tool

- ➤ Going through important Android Studio Shortcuts and Techniques

In the previous chapter, you learned how to use and refactor the most popular Android developer tools – SDK Manager, Android Virtual Device (AVD) Manager, and Navigation Editor. In this chapter, we shall break down the essentials for the Android Studio Debugging procedure. Moreover, we will show you how to navigate with Android Device Monitor and provide a list of useful shortcuts and button techniques one can apply when developing apps in Android Studio.

DOI: 10.1201/9781003229070-5   **179**

Normally, the more complex your app gets, the more likely it will contain errors. Nothing upsets a user more than an app that crashes, fails to operate under certain conditions, or gets in the way of the assignment that it was intended to accomplish. A naïve approach to development is to think that your code will always evolve along the paths you set for it. It is important to understand where your code deviates from, yet even knowing that cannot guarantee you that it shall go precisely the error-free way. And because you cannot predict all the potential faulty paths during development, it helps to develop an understanding of the various diagnostic tools and techniques involved in Android development. This chapter will explore the debugger in detail and review some other analytical tools that you can utilize to fix errors and gain insight on potential weaknesses that may hold you back as you work.

RUNNING AND DEBUGGING

Android Studio Debugger is a great tool that allows you to do the following and more:

- Choose a device to debug your app on

- Establish breakpoints in your Java, Kotlin, and C/C++ code

- Review variables and estimate expressions at runtime

However, before you can start debugging, you need to make the following simple preparations.

First things first, you begin by enabling debugging on your device. In case you are using the emulator, this must be enabled by default. But for a connected device, you need to enable debugging in the device developer options.

Once that is done, make sure to run a debuggable build variant. You should use a build variant that includes debuggable true in the build configuration. Usually, you can just pick the default "debug" variant that is included in every Android Studio project. Yet if you are going to use new build types that should be debuggable, you must add "debuggable true" to the build type as illustrated here:

```
android {
    buildTypes {
        customDebugType {
            debuggable true
            . . .
        }
```

Note that the same property also applies to modules with C/C++ code.

If your app relies on a library module that you also want to debug, that library should be packaged with debuggable true to hold its debug symbols. In order to ensure that the debuggable variants of your app project receive the debuggable variant of a library module, it is recommended to publish nondefault versions of your library.

Another thing you need to complete is setting some breakpoints in the app code. In the toolbar, pick a device to debug your app on from the target device drop-down menu. If you do not have any configured devices, you need to either connect a device via USB or create an AVD to use the Android Emulator. In the toolbar, just select the Debug option. If you see a dialog asking whether you want to "switch from Run to Debug," that means your app is already running on the device and it will restart in order to begin debugging. If you would rather keep the same instance of the app running, click Cancel Debug and instead attach the debugger to a running app.

Otherwise, Android Studio shall build an Android application package (APK), sign it with a debug key, install it on your selected device, and activate it. In case you add C and C++ code to your project, Android Studio also runs the LLDB debugger in the Debug window that is used to debug your native code. And since different debugger tools are required to debug Java/Kotlin code and C/C++ code, the Android Studio debugger lets you choose which debugger type to use. By default, Android Studio decides which debugger to apply based on which languages it tracks in your project (with the Auto debugger type). Nevertheless, you can manually select the debugger in the debug configuration (click Run > Edit Configurations) or in the dialog that pops when you click Run and Attach debugger to Android process.

There are several debug types that are most commonly used:

- **Auto:** Opt for this debug type if you need Android Studio to automatically choose the best option for the code you are debugging. For instance, if you have any C or C++ code in your project, Android Studio automatically uses the Dual debug type. Otherwise, Android Studio applies the Java debug type.

- **Java:** This debug type is most suited if you want to debug only code written in Java or Kotlin. At the same time, the Java debugger simply omits any breakpoints or watches you insert in your native code.

- **Native (Available only with C/C++ code):** This debug type is perfect if you want to use only LLDB to debug your code. When using this debug type, the Java debugger session view will not be available. By default, LLDB reviews only your native code and omits breakpoints in your Java code. Therefore, if you need to debug your Java code, you should switch to either the Auto or Dual debug type. In addition, native debugging only works on devices that meet the following requirements:

1. **The device has to support run-as:** To check whether the device supports run-as, add the following command on the ADB shell that is linked to your device:

```
run-as your-package-name pwd
```

Here, you need to replace your package name with your app's package name. If the device supports run-as, the command should return without any errors.

2. **The device has ptrace enabled:** To see whether ptrace is enabled, add the following command on the ADB shell that is linked to your device:

```
sysctl kernel.yama.ptrace_scope
```

If ptrace is enabled, the command will have the value 0 or show an unknown key error. If ptrace is not enabled, it will print any value other than 0.

3. **Dual (Available only with C/C++ code):** Dual debug type is ideal for those who need to switch between debugging both Java and native code. Android Studio attaches both the Java debugger and LLDB to your app process, one for the Java debugger and one for LLDB, so you can keep track of breakpoints in both your Java and native code without having to restart your app or change your debug configuration.

While debugging C/C++ code, you can also set special types of breakpoints, called watchpoints, that can postpone your app process when your app interacts with a particular block of memory.

To view all the breakpoints and configure breakpoint types, access the View Breakpoints on the left side of the Debug window. The Breakpoints window lets you enable or disable each breakpoint from the list of breakpoints. If a breakpoint is disabled, Android Studio does not pause your app when it encounters that breakpoint. You can configure a breakpoint to be disabled at first and have the system enable it after a different breakpoint is hit. You can also modify whether a breakpoint should be disabled after it is hit. In order to set a breakpoint for any exception, just select Exception Breakpoints in the list of breakpoints.

Debug Window Frames

In the Debugger window, the Frames function allows you to inspect the stack frame that caused the current breakpoint to be hit. This enables you to access and examine the stack frame and also inspect the list of threads in your Android app. To select a thread, use the thread selector drop-down and view its stack frame. Clicking the elements in the frame will display the source in the editor.

Inspect Variables

In the Debugger window, the Variables function lets you track variables when the system stops your app on a breakpoint and you pick a frame from the Frames pane. The Variables pane also lets you evaluate ad hoc expressions using static methods and variables available within the selected frame.

The Watches function provides similar capabilities except that expressions included in the Watches function persist between debugging sessions. You should add watches for variables and fields that you access frequently or provide a useful state for the current debugging session.

In order to add a variable or expression to the Watches list, follow these easy steps:

Once you start debugging, access the Watches function and click Add. In the text box that appears, insert the name of the variable or expression you need to watch and press Enter.

To remove an item from the Watches list, select the item and simply click Remove. It is also possible to reorder the elements in the Watches list by selecting an item and then clicking Up or Down.

Moreover, while debugging C/C++ code, you can also set watchpoints by selecting a specific variable, or to be more specific, by selecting the block of memory the system allocates to that variable, not the variable itself. This is different from adding a variable to the Watches function, enabling you to see the value of a variable but not letting you postpone your app process when the system runs or changes its value in memory.

Nevertheless, in order to set a watchpoint, you should meet the following requirements:

First, your target physical device or emulator should use an x86 or x86_64 CPU. If your device uses an ARM CPU, then you need to align the boundary of your variable's address in memory to either 4 bytes for 32-bit processors, or 8 bytes for 64-bit processors. You can align a variable in your native code by specifying __attribute__ ((aligned(num_bytes))) in the variable deceleration, just like this: int my_counter __attribute__((aligned(8)))

It is also important to remember that when your app exits a function and the system deallocates its local variables from memory, you need to reassign any watchpoints you created for those variables in order not to lose them.

View and Change Resource Value Display Format

While on the debug mode, you can view resource values and set a different display format for variables in your Java code. With the Variables tab accessed and a frame selected, go to the Variables list and right-click anywhere on a resource line to display the drop-down list. In the drop-down list, select View as and select the format you want to use.

The available formats depend on the data type of the resource you have chosen. The standard list of formats should typically include one or more of the following options:[1]

- **Class:** Display the class definition

- **toString:** Display string format

- **Object:** Display the object definition

- **Array:** Display in an array format

- **Timestamp:** Display date and time as follows: yyyy-mm-dd hh:mm:ss

- **Auto:** Android Studio chooses the best format based on the data type

- **Binary:** Display a binary value using zeroes and ones

- **MeasureSpec:** The value passed from the parent to the selected child

- **Hex:** Display as a hexadecimal value

- **Primitive:** Display as a numeric value using a primitive data type

- **Integer:** Display a numeric value of type Integer

---

[1] https://developer.android.com/studio/debug?hl=fr, Android

About Run/Debug Configurations

Run/debug configurations specify items such as app instalation, launch, and test features. You can set a configuration for one-time use, or save it for further use. Once you save it, you can access that configuration from the Select Run/Debug Configuration drop-down list within the toolbar. Android Studio saves all configurations there as part of the project.

Default Run/Debug Configuration

When you first start a project, Android Studio creates a default run/debug configuration for the main activity based on the Android App template. So to run or debug your project, you must always have at least one run/debug configuration determined in such a manner. For this reason, it is recommended that you do not remove but rather keep the default configuration.

Any run/debug configurations and template modification will apply to the current project only. In order to open the Run/Debug Configurations dialog, select the Edit

Configurations option and the Run/Debug Configurations dialog shall appear immediately. It is also possible to share your run/debug configuration (not the template) through your version control system.

The dialog presents default templates in the left panel under the Defaults folder and combines your defined configurations by template type above the Defaults folder. You can resize the dialog to look for any hidden items. In the same dialog, you can also:

- Create new run/debug configurations
- Edit run/debug configurations
- Edit default templates
- Sort and group configurations
- Create a new run/debug configuration

Also, you can establish new run/debug configurations from the Run/Debug Configurations dialog, the Project window, or the Code Editor. But the new configuration should be based on a default template.

The Run/Debug Configurations dialog displays your run/debug configurations and the available default templates. You can start a new configuration directly from a template, or from a copy of another configuration and later modify the field values as required for the project.

Alternatively, you can right-click an item in the Project window to automatically produce a configuration specific to that item. For instance, you can right-click the activity Java file and hit Run if you need to run a particular activity. Depending on the item, Android Studio applies an Android App, Android Instrumented Tests, or Android JUnit default template to create the configuration.

However, when you create a configuration outside of the Run/Debug Configurations dialog, the configuration would be treated as temporary unless you save it. By default, you can have up to five temporary configurations in the project before Android Studio starts removing them one by one. If you want to change this default, open the Run/Debug Configurations dialog and click the Defaults folder. Here you can simply type any value in the Temporary Configurations Limit field.

As already stated, for C and C++ code, Android Studio uses the LLDB debugger. In addition to the normal Android Studio user interface (UI), the debugger window has an LLDB tab that allows you to access and enter LLDB commands during debugging. You can enter the same commands that Android Studio uses to display information in the debugger UI, as well as perform any other additional operations.

Therefore, in order to add symbol directories, LLDB startup commands, in the Debugger tab you need to know how to use buttons similar to the following:[2]

- **Add** ✚ : Add a directory or command

- **Remove** ▬ : Select a directory or command and then click this button to remove the item

---

[2] https://developer.android.com/studio/run/rundebugconfig?hl=fr, Android

- **Up** : Select a directory or command and then click this button to move the item up in the list

- **Down** : Select a directory or command and then click this button to move the item down in the list

Once you have selected which Debug type to go with:

- **Java:** Debug Java code only

- **Auto:** Let Android Studio choose the best debug type for your project

- **Native:** Debug native C or C++ cod

- **Dual:** Debug Java and native code in two separate debug sessions

You can now move onto including extra components in your project, starting from components that we have just mentioned: symbol directories and LLBD commands.

Symbol Directories

If you want to add symbol files to provide the debugger with C or C++ information generated outside of Android Studio, you can add one or more symbol directories. Android Studio preferentially registers any files within these directories over files generated by the Android Plugin for Gradle. The debugger looks for symbol directories from top to bottom, in order, until it finds what it needs. It also searches recursively through the files in the directory. Thus, in order to optimize the list and save your time, you can put the directories used most often toward the top of the list.

When you specify a directory high in the tree, it can take longer to search all of the subdirectories. But if you add a very specific directory, it takes less time to search. You need to find the right balance between speed and finding the files you need for debugging. For instance, if you have a directory that holds subdirectories for different Android Binary Interfaces (ABIs), you can add a directory for a specific ABI or for all ABIs. It might take longer to search through the upper-level directory, but at the same time, it is also more secure if you decide to debug on a different device.

Remember that there is no need to add directories containing Gradle symbol files because the debugger uses them automatically.

LLDB Startup Commands

Add LLDB commands that you want to run before the debugger attaches to the process. For example, you can identify settings for the environment, as shown in the following command:

```
settings set target.max-memory-read-size
2048
```

LLDB runs the commands in order from top to bottom.

LLDB Post Attach Commands

Add LLDB commands that you need to run right after the debugger attaches to the process. To illustrate:

```
process handle SIGPIPE -n true -p true -s
false
```

LLDB runs the commands in order from top to bottom.

Logging: Target Channels

Target channels are mostly applied to specify LLDB log options. Android Studio sets the default options based on your requirements—so it is not too slow but has needed information for troubleshooting issues. The log may also be often requested for Android Studio bug reports. The default feature is

```
lldb process:gdb-remote packets
```

However, it is also possible to change the default to gather more information. For example, the following log options gather information about a specific platform:

```
lldb process platform:gdb-remote packets
```

Android Studio places device logs in the following location, where ApplicationId is the unique application ID that is used in your built APK manifest and identifies your app on your device and in the Google Play Store:

/data/data/ApplicationId/lldb/log

Similarly, when multiple users access a device, it places the logs in the following location, where AndroidUserId is a unique identifier for a user on the device:

/data/user/AndroidUserId/ApplicationId/lldb/log

Miscellaneous Tab

The Miscellaneous tab is mostly used to specify logcat, installation, launch, and deployment options:

- **Logcat:** Clear log before launch
  Select this option if you need Android Studio to delete all data from previous sessions from the log

file before starting the app. By default, this option is deselected.

- **Installation Options:** Skip installation if APK has not changed
  When selected, Android Studio does not redeploy your APK if it detects that it is unmodified. If you want Android Studio to force an install of the APK, even if it has not changed, then deselect this option because by default it stays selected.

- **Installation Options:** Force stop running application before launching activity
  If selected, when Android Studio detects that it does not have to reinstall an APK because it has not changed, it will force-stop the app to start from the default launcher activity. If this option is deselected, Android Studio will not force-stop the app. This option works in conjunction with the previous option that regulates whether an APK is installed or not. It is better for both Installation Options fields to leave them at the default unless you explicitly want to force an install every time.

In some cases, you might need to deselect this option. For instance, if you are writing an input method engine (IME), force-stopping the app deselects it as the current keyboard, which might not suit your plans.

ANDROID DEVICE MONITOR

Android Device Monitor is a stand-alone tool that offers a graphical UI for several Android application debugging and analysis services. The Monitor tool does not require the installation of an integrated development environment and encapsulates the following tools: Dalvik Debug Monitor Server, Traceview, Systrace, Hierarchy Viewer, Pixel Perfect, and Network Traffic tool.

To start the standalone Device Monitor application in Android Studio 3.1 and lower, insert the following on the command line in the android-SDK/tools/directory:

monitor

You can then link the tool to a connected device by picking it from the Devices pane. But if you have trouble viewing functions or windows, try editing with the Reset Perspective function from the menu bar.

Now let's go through the main Android Device Monitor components that were mentioned earlier.

Dalvik Debug Monitor Server (DDMS)

This tool is deprecated. Instead, you should use Android Profiler (since Android Studio 3.0 and higher) to profile your app's CPU, memory, and network manipulations.

The Android Profiler tools offer real-time data to help you recognize how your app uses CPU, memory, network, and battery potential. Great features provided by advanced profiling include the following:

- Setting event timeline on all profiler windows

- Tracking the number of allocated objects in Memory Profiler

- Activating garbage collection events in Memory Profiler

- Providing information about all transmitted files in Network Profiler

Keep in mind that all of these features are available to you by default if your device is running Android 8.0 or higher.

To enable advanced profiling, simply select Run and Edit Configurations. Here, click on your app module and then check Enable advanced profiling. The advanced profiling configuration makes the build process slower, so you should enable it only when you truly need to start profiling your app.

If you want to perform other debugging tasks, such as forwarding commands to a connected device to set up port-forwarding, transfer files, or take screenshots, then you can use the Android Debug Bridge (ADB), Android Emulator, or Debugger window.

Traceview

This tool is also deprecated. Thus, if you want to inspect. trace files resulted from instrumenting your app with the Debug class and recording new method traces, simply use the Android Studio CPU profiler.

Systrace

In case you need to inspect native system processes and forward UI jank caused by dropped frames, apply systrace from the command line or the simplified System Trace in the CPU Profiler.

You can use the CPU Profiler to inspect your app's CPU usage and thread activity in real-time while interacting with your app, or you can review the details in recorded method traces, function traces, and system traces.

The specific kinds of data that the CPU Profiler registers and shows are determined by which recording configuration you select:[3]

- **System trace:** Captures fine-grained items that let you inspect how your app interacts with system resources.

- **Method and function traces:** For each thread in your app process, you can track which methods (Java) or functions (C/C++) are implemented over a period of time and the CPU resources each method or function requests during its execution. You can also use method and function traces to identify callers and callees. A caller here could be defined as a method or function that activates another method or function, and a callee is one that is invoked by another method or function. You can use this information to see which methods or functions are responsible for calling particular resource-heavy activities too often and optimize your app's code to avoid unnecessary load.

In addition, the default view for the CPU Profiler includes the following timelines:

- **Event timeline:** Displays various activities in your app as they go through different stages in their lifecycle, and indicates user interactions with the device, including screen rotation events.

- **CPU timeline:** Provides real-time CPU usage of your app—as a percentage of total available CPU time—and the total number of threads your app is running. The timeline also displays the CPU usage

---

[3] https://developer.android.com/studio/profile/monitor, Android

of other processes (such as system processes or other apps), so you can compare it to your app's usage. You can inspect historical CPU usage data by simply moving your mouse along the horizontal axis of the timeline.

Thread activity timeline: Reviews each thread that belongs to your app process and indicates their activity along a timeline using the colors listed below. After you register a trace, you can select a thread from this timeline to inspect its data in the trace function.

- **Green:** The thread is active or is ready to use the CPU. Meaning that it is in a running or runnable state.

- **Yellow:** The thread is active, but it is waiting for an I/O operation, such as disk or network I/O, before it can complete its work.

- **Gray:** The thread is not active and is not consuming any CPU time. This sometimes occurs when the thread requires access to a resource that is not yet available. Either the thread goes into voluntary sleep, or the kernel puts the thread to sleep until the required resource becomes available.

Hierarchy Viewer

Since this tool is also deprecated, you should use Layout Inspector to inspect your app's view hierarchy at runtime.

The Layout Inspector in Android Studio lets you compare your app layout with other standard design mockups, display a magnified or 3D view of your app, as well as examine details of its layout at runtime. This is particularly convenient when your layout is built at runtime rather than entirely in XML; therefore, could be behaving unexpectedly at times.

In addition, the Layout Validation feature allows you to simultaneously preview layouts on different devices and show configurations, including variable font sizes or user languages, making it easy to run tests for a variety of common layout issues. In order to open the Layout Inspector, start your app on a connected device or emulator and access Tools, then Layout Inspector. Typically, Layout Inspector should display the following components:

- **Component Tree:** The hierarchy of views in the layout

- **Layout Display:** Rendering of app layout as it appears on your device or emulator, with layout bounds shown for each view

- **Layout Inspector toolbar:** Tools for the Layout Inspector

- **Attributes:** The layout attributes for the selected view

Pixel Perfect

Similar to other tools, Pixel Perfect has also been deprecated. If you need to work on design mockups, make sure to use Layout Inspector.

Network Traffic Tool

Similar to other tools, the Network traffic tool is also deprecated. In case you need to view how and when your app transmits data over a network, we recommend using the Network Profiler instead. The Network Profiler provides real-time network activity on a timeline, showing data forwarded and received, as well as the current number of connections. This allows you to examine how and when your app manipulates data, and optimize the underlying code appropriately.

There might be some doubts about why you should register and profile your app's network activity at all. This is quite unnecessary. Think about this instead – when your app sends a request to the network, the device must use the power-hungry mobile or WiFi radios to forward and receive packets. The radios use power to transfer data and use extra power to turn on and stay awake.

Using the Network Profiler, you will be able to look for frequent, short spikes of network activity, which means that your app requires the radios to turn on frequently or stay awake for long periods to administer many short requests close together. This pattern shows that you may be able to optimize your app for better battery performance by batching network requests, thereby minimizing the number of times the radios must turn on to send or receive data. This also lets the radios switch into low-power mode to save battery in the long gaps between batched requests.

In order to open the Network Profiler, go to the Tool Windows and click on Profiler. Make sure to select the device and app process you want to profile from the Android Profiler toolbar. If you have connected a device over USB but cannot find it listed, ensure that you have enabled USB debugging.

Also, if you want to select a portion of the timeline, inspect a list of network requests sent and responses received, or check detailed information about a selected file, you should enable advanced profiling first.

IMPORTANT SHORTCUTS AND BUTTON TECHNIQUES

Android Studio has various keyboard shortcuts for many common actions. In this section, we shall list multiple defaults as well as specific to some operation keyboard shortcuts. In addition to the keymaps you will see here, you can also select necessary features from preset keymaps or even create a custom keymap yourself. Keep in mind, because Android Studio is based on IntelliJ IDEA, you can find additional shortcuts in the IntelliJ IDEA keymap reference documentation: https://resources.jetbrains.com/storage/products/intellij-idea/docs/IntelliJIDEA_ReferenceCard.pdf

Default keyboard shortcuts presented here come with Windows/Linux and Mac operating systems options.[4]

General

1. Save all – Control+S/Command+S

2. Synchronize – Control+Alt+Y/Command+Option+Y

3. Maximize/minimize editor – Control+Shift+F12/Control+Command+F12

4. Add to favorites – Alt+Shift+F/Option+Shift+F

---

[4] https://developer.android.com/studio/intro/keyboard-shortcuts, Android

5. Inspect current file with current profile – Alt+Shift+I/Option+Shift+I

6. Quick switch scheme – Control+` (backquote)/Control+` (backquote)

7. Open settings dialogue – Control+Alt+S/Command+, (comma)

8. Open project structure dialog – Control+Alt+Shift+S/Command+; (semicolon)

9. Switch between tabs and tool window – Control+Tab/Control+Tab

Navigating and Searching Within Studio

1. Search everything (including code and menus) – Press Shift twice/Press Shift twice

2. Find – Control+F/Command+F

3. Find next – F3/Command+G

4. Find previous – Shift+F3/Command+Shift+G

5. Replace – Control+R/Command+R

6. Find action – Control+Shift+A/Command+Shift+A

7. Search by symbol name – Control+Alt+Shift+N/Command+Option+O

8. Find class – Control+N/Command+O

9. Find file (instead of class) – Control+Shift+N/Command+Shift+O

10. Find in path – Control+Shift+F/Command+Shift+F

11. Open file structure pop-up – Control+F12/ Command+F12

12. Navigate between open editor tabs – Alt+Right Arrow or Left Arrow/Control+Right Arrow or Control+Left Arrow

13. Jump to source – F4 or Control+Enter/F4 or Command+Down Arrow

14. Open current editor tab in new window – Shift+F4/ Shift+F4

15. Recently opened files pop-up – Control+E/ Command+E

16. Recently edited files pop-up – Control+Shift+E/ Command+Shift+E

17. Go to last edit location – Control+Shift+Backspace/ Command+Shift+Delete

18. Close active editor tab – Control+F4/Command+W

19. Return to editor window from a tool window – Esc/ Esc

20. Hide active or last active tool window – Shift+Esc/ Shift+Esc

21. Go to line – Control+G/Command+L

22. Open type hierarchy – Control+H/Control+H

23. Open method hierarchy – Control+Shift+H/ Command+Shift+H

24. Open call hierarchy – Control+Alt+H/ Control+Option+H

Viewing Layouts

1. Zoom in/out – Control+plus or Control+minus/ Command+plus or Command+minus

2. Fit to screen –Control+0/Command+0

3. Actual size – Control+Shift+1/Command+Shift+1

Design Tools: Layout Editor

1. Toggle between Design and Blueprint modes – B/B

2. Toggle between Portrait and Landscape modes – O/O

3. Toggle devices – D/D

4. Force refresh – R/R

5. Toggle render errors panel –E/E

6. Delete constraints – Delete or Control+click/Delete or Command+click

7. Zoom in – Control+plus/Command+plus

8. Zoom out – Control+minus/Command+minus

9. Zoom to fit – Control+0/Command+0

10. Pan – Hold Space+click and drag/Hold Space+click and drag

11. Go to XML – Control+B/Command+B

12. Select all components – Control+A/Command+A

13. Select multiple components – Shift+click or Control+click/Shift+click or Command+click

Design Tools: Navigation Editor

1. Zoom in – Control+plus/Command+plus

2. Zoom out – Control+minus/Command+minus

3. Zoom to fit – Control+0/Command+0

4. Pan – Hold Space+click and drag/Hold Space+click and drag

5. Go to XML – Control+B/Command+B

6. Toggle render errors panel –E/E

7. Group into a nested graph – Control+G/Command+G

8. Cycle through destinations – Tab or Shift+Tab/Tab or Shift+Tab

9. Select all destinations – Control+A/Command+A

10. Select multiple destinations – Shift+click or Control+click/Shift+click or Command+click

Writing Code

1. Generate code (getters, setters, constructors, hashCode/equals, toString, new file, new class) – Alt+Insert/Command+N

2. Override methods – Control+O/Control+O

3. Implement methods – Control+I/Control+I

4. Surround with (if … else/try … catch) – Control+Alt+T/ Command+Option+T

5. Delete line at caret – Control+Y/Command+Delete

6. Collapse/expand current code block – Control+ minus or Control+plus/Command+minus or Command+plus

7. Collapse/expand all code blocks – Control+Shift+ minus or Control+Shift+plus/Command+Shift+ minus or Command+Shift+plus

8. Duplicate current line or selection – Control+D/ Command+D

9. Basic code completion – Control+Space/Control+ Space

10. Smart code completion (filters the list of methods and variables by expected type) – Control+Shift+Space/ Control+Shift+Space

11. Complete statement – Control+Shift+Enter/ Command+Shift+Enter

12. Quick documentation lookup – Control+Q/Control+J

13. Show parameters for selected method – Control+P/ Command+P

14. Go to declaration (directly) – Control+B or Control+click/Command+B or Command+click

15. Go to implementations – Control+Alt+B/ Command+Option+B

16. Go to super-method/super-class – Control+U/ Command+U

17. Open quick definition lookup – Control+Shift+I/ Command+Y

18. Toggle project tool window visibility – Alt+1/ Command+1

19. Toggle bookmark – F11/F3

20. Toggle bookmark with mnemonic – Control+F11/ Option+F3

21. Comment/uncomment with line comment – Control+//Command+/

22. Comment/uncomment with block comment – Control+Shift+//Command+Shift+/

23. Select successively increasing code blocks – Control+W/Option+Up

24. Decrease current selection to previous state – Control+Shift+W/Option+Down

25. Move to code block start – Control+[/ Option+Command+[

26. Move to code block end – Control+]/ Option+Command+]

27. Select to the code block start – Control+Shift+[/ Option+Command+Shift+[

28. Select to the code block end – Control+Shift+]/
Option+Command+Shift+]

29. Delete to end of word – Control+Delete/Option+Delete

30. Delete to start of word – Control+Backspace/
Option+Delete

31. Optimize imports – Control+Alt+O/
Control+Option+O

32. Project quick fix (show intention actions and quick
fixes) – Alt+Enter/Option+Enter

33. Reformat code – Control+Alt+L/
Command+Option+L

34. Auto-indent lines – Control+Alt+I/Control+Option+I

35. Indent/unindent lines – Tab or Shift+Tab/Tab or
Shift+Tab

36. Smart line join – Control+Shift+J/Control+Shift+J

37. Smart line split – Control+Enter/Command+Enter

38. Start new line – Shift+Enter/Shift+Enter

39. Next/previous highlighted error – F2 or Shift+F2/F2
or Shift+F2

Build and Run

1. Build – Control+F9/Command+F9

2. Build and run – Shift+F10/Control+R

3. Apply Changes and Restart Activity – Control+F10/ Control+Command+R

4. Apply Code Changes – Control+Alt+F10/Control+ Shift+Command+R

Debugging

1. Debug – Shift+F9/Control+D

2. Step over – F8/F8

3. Step into – F7/F7

4. Smart step into – Shift+F7/Shift+F7

5. Step out – Shift+F8/Shift+F8

6. Run to cursor – Alt+F9/Option+F9

7. Evaluate expression – Alt+F8/Option+F8

8. Resume program – F9/Command+Option+R

9. Toggle breakpoint – Control+F8/Command+F8

10. View breakpoints – Control+Shift+F8/Command+ Shift+F8

Refactoring

1. Copy – F5/F5

2. Move – F6/F6

3. Safe delete – Alt+Delete/Command+Delete

4. Rename – Shift+F6/Shift+F6

5. Change signature – Control+F6/Command+F6

6. Inline – Control+Alt+N/Command+Option+N

7. Extract method – Control+Alt+M/Command+ Option+M

8. Extract variable – Control+Alt+V/Command+ Option+V

9. Extract field – Control+Alt+F/Command+Option+F

10. Extract constant – Control+Alt+C/Command+ Option+C

11. Extract parameter – Control+Alt+P/Command+ Option+P

Version Control/Local History

1. Commit project to VCS – Control+K/Command+K

2. Update project from VCS – Control+T/Command+T

3. View recent changes – Alt+Shift+C/Option+Shift+C

4. Open VCS popup – Alt+` (backquote)/Control+V

No, we shall look through the Android SDK key short-cuts and commands that are composed of multiple packages required for app development. Here we are going to list the most important command-line tools that are available, organized by the packages in which they are delivered.

You can install and edit each package using Android Studio's SDK Manager or the SDK manager command-line tool. All of the packages are available by default through your Android SDK directory, which you can access as follows: In Android Studio, click File and open Project Structure where everything is located.[5] At the same time, you can have multiple versions of the build tools to build your app for different Android versions.

- **apkanalyzer:** Offers insight into the composition of your APK after the build process completes.

- **avdmanager:** Lets you create and manage AVDs from the command line.

- **lint:** Invokes a code scanning tool that can help you to identify and correct problems with the structural quality of your code.

- **retrace:** For applications compiled by R8, retrace decodes an obfuscated stack trace that maps back to your original source code.

- **sdkmanager:** Allows you to view, install, update, and uninstall packages for the Android SDK.
  In addition to the above mentioned, there are also certain SDK Build Tools that are located in: android_sdk/build-tools/version/. These are mainly required to build Android apps. Most of the tools in this package are invoked by the build tools and not intended

---

[5] https://developer.android.com/studio/command-line?hl=th, Android

for you. However, the following command-line tools might be useful:

- **aapt2:** Parses, indexes, and compiles Android resources into a binary format that is optimized for the Android platform, and packages the compiled resources into a single output.

- **apksigner:** Signs APKs and checks whether APK signatures will be verified successfully on all platform versions that a given APK supports.

- **zipalign:** Optimizes APK files by ensuring that all uncompressed data starts with a particular alignment relative to the start of the file.

  In Android SDK, apart from the Build Tools, certain Platform Tools are located in: android_sdk/platform-tools/. These tools are updated for every new version of the Android platform to serve new features (and sometimes more often to test and update the tools), and each update is backward compatible with older platform versions.

- **adb:** Android Debug Bridge (ADB) is a versatile tool that lets you organize the state of an emulator instance or Android-powered device. You can also use it to install an APK on a device.

- **etcltool:** A command-line utility that allows you to encode PNG images to the ETC1 compression standard and decode ETC1 compressed images back to PNG.

- **fastboot:** Used to flash a device with the platform and other system images.

- **logcat:** This is a tool invoked via ADB to view app and system logs.

Another important Android build tool that should be discussed in AAPT2 or Android Asset Packaging Tool that Android Studio and Android Gradle Plugin utilize to collect and package your app's resources. AAPT2 parses, indexes, and compiles the resources into a binary format that is optimized for the Android platform. In order to apply AAPT2 from the command line on Linux or Mac, simply run the aapt2 command. On Windows, you should insert the aapt2. exe command. AAPT2 supports faster compilation of data by enabling incremental compilation. This is achieved by breaking resource processing into two following steps:

a. **Compile:** compiles resource files into binary formats.

b. **Link:** merges all compiled files and packages them into a single package.

Compile Options

There are several key commands that you can use with the compile command, as shown below:[6]

- **o path:** Specifies the output path for the compiled resources. This is a mandatory flag because you have

---

[6] https://developer.android.com/studio/command-line/aapt2?hl=th, Android

to specify a path to a directory where AAPT2 can output and place the compiled resources.

- **dir directory:** Specifies the directory to scan for resources. Although you can use this flag to collect multiple resource files with one command, it disables the advantages of incremental compilation and thus, should not be applied for large projects.

- **pseudo-localize:** Used to generate pseudo-localized versions of default strings, such as en-XA and en-XB.

- **no-crunch:** Activated to disable PNG processing. You can use this option if you have already processed the PNG files, or if you are creating debug builds that do not need file size reduction. Enabling this option results in faster execution, but increases the output file size.

- **legacy:** Treats errors that are permissible when using earlier versions of AAPT as warnings. Also, this flag is suitable for unexpected compile-time errors too.

- **v:** Used to enable verbose logging.

Link Options

You can use the following options with the link command:[7]

- **o path:** Specifies the output path for the linked resource APK. This is a mandatory link flag because

---

[7] https://developer.android.com/studio/command-line/aapt2?hl=th, Android

you are expected to specify the path for the output APK that can hold the linked resources.

- **manifest file:** Used to specify the path to the Android manifest file to build. This is another mandatory flag because the manifest file holds essential information about your app like package name and application ID.

- **I:** This command provides the path to the platform's android.jar or other APKs like framework-res.apk which might be useful while building features. This flag is necessary if you are using attributes with android namespace (for instance, android:id) in your resource files.

- **A directory:** This directory specifies assets to be included in the APK. You can also use this directory to store original unprocessed files.

- **R file:** Applied to forward individual .flat file to link, using overlay semantics without using the <add-resource> tag. When you provide a resource file that overlays, extends, or modifies an existing file, the last conflicting resource given is used.

- **package-id:** Specifies the package ID to use for your app. The package ID that you specify must be greater than or equal to 0x7f unless used in combination with allow-reserved-package-id.

- **allow-reserved-package-id:** Allows the use of a reserved package ID. Reserved package IDs are IDs that are typpically assigned to shared libraries and are in the range from 0x02 to 0x7e inclusive. By inserting -allow-reserved-package-id, you can assign IDs that fall in the range of reserved package IDs. This should only be used for packages with a min-SDK version of 26 or lower.

- **java directory:** Specifies the directory in which to generate R.java.

- **proguard proguard_options:** Produces output file for ProGuard rules.

- **proguard-conditional-keep-rules:** Produces output file for ProGuard rules for the main dex.

- **no-auto-version:** Disables automatic style and layout SDK versioning.

- **no-version-vectors:** Disables automatic versioning of vector drawables. Apply this only when building your APK with the Vector Drawable Library.

- **no-version-transitions:** Disables automatic versioning of transition resources. Use this only when building your APK with the Transition Support library.

- **no-resource-deduping:** Disables automatic de-duplication of resources with identical values across compatible configurations.

- **enable-sparse-encoding:** Used to enable encoding of sparse entries using a binary search tree. This is particularly useful for optimization of APK size but at the cost of resource retrieval performance.

- **z:** Used to request localization of strings marked 'suggested'.

- **c config:** Provides a list of configurations separated by commas. For instance, if you have dependencies on the support library which holds translations for multiple languages, you can filter resources just for the given language configuration, like English or Spanish.

  You are typically advised to define the language configuration by a two-letter ISO 639-1 language code, optionally followed by a two-letter ISO 3166-1-alpha-2 region code preceded by lowercase 'r' (for example, en-rUS).

- **preferred-density:** Allows AAPT2 to choose the closest matching density and strip out all others. Several pixel density qualifiers are available to use in your app, such as ldpi, hdpi, and xhdpi. When selecting a preferred density, AAPT2 will store the closest matching density in the resource table and remove all others.

- **output-to-dir:** Outputs the APK contents to a directory specified by -o. If you get any errors with this flag, you can resolve them by upgrading to Android SDK Build Tools 28.0.0 or higher.

- **min-SDK-version:** Sets the default minimum SDK version to use for AndroidManifest.xml.

- **target-SDK-version:** Sets the default target SDK version to use for AndroidManifest.xml.

- **version-code:** Specifies the version code to insert into the AndroidManifest.xml if none is present.

- **compile-SDK-version-name:** Identifies the version name to insert into the AndroidManifest.xml if none is present.

- **proto-format:** Produces compiled resources in Protobuf format. Applicable as input to the bundle tool for creating Android App Bundle.

- **nonfinal-ids:** Results in R.java with nonfinal resource IDs (references to the IDs from app's code that do not get inlined during kotlinc/javac compilation).

- **emit-ids path:** Emits a file at the given path with a list of names of resource types and their ID mappings. Mostly suited to use with –stable-ids.

- **stable-ids outputfilename.ext:** Contains the file generated with –emit-ids that holds the list of names of resource types and their assigned IDs. This option permits assigned IDs to remain stable even when you remove or add new resources during linking.

- **custom-package package_name:** Identifies custom Java package under which to produce R.java.

- **extra-packages package_name:** Produces the same R.java file but with different package names.

- **add-Javadoc-annotation:** Adds a JavaDoc annotation to all generated Java classes.

- **output-text-symbols path:** Produces a text file containing the resource symbols of the R class in the specified file. You are expected to specify the path to the output file.

- **auto-add-overlay:** Permits the addition of new resources in overlays without using the <add-resource> tag.

- **rename-manifest-package:** Renames the package in AndroidManifest.xml.

- **rename-instrumentation-target-package:** Changes the name of the target package for instrumentation. It typically should be used in addition to -rename-manifest-package.

- **0 extension:** Used to specify the extensions of files that you do not need to compress.

- **split path:config[,config[..]]:** Splits resources based on a set of configurations to create a different version of the APK. You should specify the path to the output APK together with the set of configurations.

- **v:** Used to enable increased verbosity of the output.

Environment Variables

In order to specify things like where the SDK is installed and where user-specific data is stored, you should know how to set environment variables for Android Studio and the command-line tools.

The following example illustrates how to use an environment variable to launch an emulator when the SDK installation has been put in E:\Android\sdk\instead of in its default location of $USER_HOME or $HOME:

$ set ANDROID_SDK_ROOT=E:\Android\sdk\
$ emulator -and Pixel_API_25

Now let's see what are the most commonly used environment variables for the Android SDK tools:[8]

- **ANDROID_SDK_ROOT:** Used to set the path to the SDK installation directory. Once set, the value does not usually change, and can be shared by multiple users on the same machine. ANDROID_HOME, which also points to the SDK installation directory, is permanently deprecated. But if you still continue to use it, the following rules will automatically apply:

  If ANDROID_HOME is included and has a valid SDK installation, its value is used instead of the value in ANDROID_SDK_ROOT. But if ANDROID_HOME is not determined, the value in ANDROID_SDK_ROOT is used. If ANDROID_HOME is defined but does not exist or does not hold a valid SDK installation, the value in ANDROID_SDK_ROOT is used instead.

- **REPO_OS_OVERRIDE:** Remember to use this variable to windows, macosx, or Linux when you use SDK manager to download packages for an operating system different from the current machine.

---

[8] https://developer.android.com/studio/command-line/variables?hl=fr, Android

Android Studio Configuration Environment Variables

The Android Studio configuration variables consist of settings that customize the location of configuration files and the JDK. To start with, check the following variables for settings:

- **STUDIO_VM_OPTIONS:** Identifies the location of the studio.vmoptions file. This file holds settings that affect the performance characteristics of the Java HotSpot Virtual Machine.

- **STUDIO_PROPERTIES:** Used to set the location of the idea.properties file. This file lets you customize Android Studio IDE properties, such as the path to user-installed plugins, and the maximum file size supported by the IDE.

- **STUDIO_JDK:** Identifies the location of the JDK with which to run Android Studio. Once you launch the IDE, it checks the STUDIO_JDK, JDK_HOME, and JAVA_HOME environment variables in that order.

- **STUDIO_GRADLE_JDK:** Used to set the location of the JDK that Android Studio uses to start the Gradle daemon. Once you launch the IDE, it first checks STUDIO_GRADLE_JDK. If STUDIO_GRADLE_JDK is not defined, the IDE applies the value set in the Project Structure dialog.

Emulator Environment Variables

By default, the emulator keeps configuration files under $HOME/.android/ and AVD data under $HOME/.android/

avd/. It is possible to modify the defaults by setting the following environment variables. The emulator -avd <avd_name> command searches the avd directory in the order of the values in $ANDROID_AVD_HOME, $ANDROID_SDK_HOME/. android/avd/, and $HOME/. android/avd/.

Worth noting that starting from Android Studio 4.2, the ANDROID_SDK_HOME environment variable is deprecated and has been replaced with ANDROID_PREFS_ROOT.

- **ANDROID_EMULATOR_HOME:** Used to establish the path to the user-specific emulator configuration directory. In Android Studio 4.1 and lower, the default location is $ANDROID_SDK_HOME/. android/. However, starting with Android Studio 4.2, the ANDROID_SDK_HOME environment variable is deprecated and the default location of the emulator configuration directory is now $ANDROID_PREFS_ROOT/.android/.

- **ANDROID_AVD_HOME:** Creates the path to the directory that holds all AVD-specific files, which mostly consist of very large disk images. The default location is $ANDROID_EMULATOR_HOME/avd/. You might want to specify a new location if the default location is low on disk space.

  In addition, the Android emulator requires the following environment variables when it starts:

- **HTTP_PROXY:** Holds the HTTP/HTTPS proxy (hostname and port) setting for a global

HTTP proxy. Uses a colon (:) separator between the host and the port. For instance, you can set HTTP_PROXY=myserver:1981.

- **ANDROID_EMULATOR_USE_SYSTEM_LIBS:** Contains a value of 0 (default) or 1. A value of 1 means to use the system's libstdc++.so file instead of the one that comes with the emulator. You should set this environment variable only when the emulator does not start on your Linux system due to a potential library problem. For instance, when some Linux Radeon GL driver libraries require a more recent libstdc++.so file.

adb Environment Variables

- **ANDROID_SERIAL:** You need to use this variable to provide an emulator serial number, such as emulator-5555, to an ADB command. In case you set this variable, but use the -s option to identify a serial number from the command line, the command-line input overrides the value in ANDROID_SERIAL.

The following example sets ANDROID_SERIAL and calls adb install helloworld.apk, which then installs the APK on emulator-5555:

```
set ANDROID_SERIAL=emulator-555
adb install helloWorld.apk
```

ADB Logcat Environment Variables

- **ANDROID_LOG_TAGS:** You can use this environment variable to establish a default filter expression when you are running logcat from your development computer. To illustrate with an example:

```
set ANDROID_LOG_TAGS=ActivityManager:I
MyApp:D *:.
```

- **ADB_TRACE:** Consist of a comma-separated list of the debug information to log. Default values can be the following: all, adb, sockets, packets, rwx, USB, sync, sysdeps, transport, and JDWP. In order to display the ADB logs for the ADB clients and the ADB server, make sure to set ADB_TRACE to all, and then call the ADB logcat command, as demonstrated here:

```
set ADB_TRACE=all
ADB logcat
```

- **ANDROID_VERBOSE:** Contains a comma-separated list of verbose output options used by the emulator. The following example shows ANDROID_VERBOSE defined with the debug-socket and debug-radio debug tags:

```
set ANDROID_VERBOSE=socket,radio
```

How to Set Environment Variables

At last, let's see how you should set environment variables in a terminal window and in a shell script for different operating systems. Keep in mind that variable settings in terminal windows last as long as the window is open while variable settings in shell scripts remain across all login sessions.

For Windows: access the terminal window and simply type the following:

```
set HTTP_PROXY=myserver:1981
```

Alternately, you can add the same command into a shell script through the Windows UI.

If you are running on Mac and Linux: similarly open a terminal window, and type the following:

```
export HTTP_PROXY=myserver:1981
```

To conclude, this chapter explored the various tools available to analyze and design your application. It looked at the many options available for exploring your app's performance from different aspects. You learned to use the new Android Device Monitor to quickly test ideas that can later be built into fully-fledged applications. Finally, you went into depth on the Android Studio Debugging procedure and saw how to use multiple key shortcuts and button techniques when developing apps in Android Studio. Each of these tools should give you powerful control and insight that can be practiced to build robust applications.

Appraisal

If you strive to become an Android Developer, then you have made an excellent choice with this book. We believe that Android will continue to consolidate its dominant global market position for several simple reasons. First, Android's modular architecture is perfect for a wide variety of configurations and customizations. Second, all the core applications that ship standard with Android devices are interchangeable with any number of third-party applications. And at last, Android Studio is considered revolutionary in the field because it streamlines the Android development process and makes Android development far more accessible than it has ever been.

It is best to view Android as a technology platform with its own ecosystem of tools to maintain it. After Android Studio, the next most important tool in the Android ecosystem is Git. It is a distributed source-control tool that is quickly becoming the standard not only for mobile development, but for software engineering in general. Git could very well be the subject of another book, but fortunately you do not need to understand all of Git's functionality to be proficient at using it. Android Studio has a great integrated and full-featured Git tool with an impressive user interface. In this book, we have covered the built-in Git features you need to know to be an effective Android Studio user and then pointed you to resources for additional research if you wish to deepen your knowledge of this tool independently.

Another important tool in the Android ecosystem is Gradle. It is best defined as a build tool similar to Ant and Maven that lets you administer libraries and library projects, run instrumentation tests, as well as manage conditional builds. And even though Android Studio does a good job of managing libraries all on its own, Gradle simply makes this task easy and portable. As with Git, Gradle is fully integrated into Android Studio, which ships with an impressive array of views that allow you to inspect Gradle files graphically and examine the output of a Gradle build process.

The Gradle build system is a general tool for building software packages from a collection of source files. It holds some high-level concepts for building software that are consistent for most projects. Moreover, Gradle Android projects have a unique hierarchical structure that nests subprojects or modules in individual folders under the project root. The most common structural components include projects, source sets, build artifacts, dependency artifacts, and repositories. Now, a project stands for a location on your hard drive that has a collection of all the project source code. A Gradle build will have a set of source files that are represented as source sets. It will typically include list of dependencies. These dependencies are software artifacts that can include anything from JAR or ZIP archives to text files, to precompiled binary files. These artifacts are delivered from a repository. And a repository is nothing but a collection of artifacts that are organized in a special way to let the build system find a given artifact. It can be a location on your hard drive or a special web site that organizes artifacts by a standard convention. Each artifact can optionally include its own set of dependencies that may be included in the build. The build can also publish these artifacts to a repository to make them available for other developers or teams.

In case you think that you would be able to develop Android apps in Android Studio without having a good understanding of Java, you will be frustrated. Java is an extremely helpful and popular programming language for many reasons. Perhaps the most important reason for Java's popularity is that Java is memory managed. Memory managed means that the programmer does not need to be dealing with deallocating memory off the heap, nor with worrying about memory leaks. Therefore, programmers developing in a memory-managed environment tend to be more productive, and their programs typically have fewer runtime errors. Just like Java, Android Studio is a memory-managed programming environment. Managing memory turned out to be such a great idea that both Microsoft and Apple have adopted this model for their mobile development platforms.

The process of creating apps or any software has historically involved writing code in a particular programming language and then compiling that code into an executable form. Android Studio uses its knowledge of object-oriented programming to generate extremely relevant and well-formed code. Features covered in this book include overriding methods, surrounding statements with Java blocks, using templates to insert code, using auto-completion, commenting code, and moving code. If your goal is to truly master Android Studio, you will be pleased with the variety of tools and techniques described here in attempt to positively affect your programming productivity.

However, keep in mind that the solutions you develop in Android Studio will not always follow a straight path from design to finish. In order to be a successful Android programmer, you need to be flexible and refactor your code as you develop, debug, and test. The greatest risk when working with code is that you may introduce unintended errors. Android Studio prevents these risks by analyzing the consequences of certain refactoring processes, and then activates the Find tool window, in which you may preview your changes—flagged with any errors or conflicts—before carrying them out.

Many of the refactoring operations presented in this book can also be performed without Android Studio's tools. Nevertheless, you should avoid operating by brute force (for example, by resorting to a global find-and-replace option) because Android Studio cannot always save you from introducing errors in those circumstances. In contrast, if Android Studio detects that you might be attempting a refactoring operation, it will try to prevent you from making any crucial mistakes. For instance, the move operation, which analyzes the consequences of your move procedures, allows you to preview the changes, and then gracefully changes any import statements for that class throughout your entire project to the new fully qualified package name.

At the same time, modern software development involves not only linking and compilation but also testing, packaging, and gradual distribution of your end product. A build system fills these essential needs by providing the necessary tools to accomplish these tasks. Consider the list of key requirements many developers face today: supporting variations of the end product (a debug version, a release version, a paid version, and a free version), managing third-party software libraries and items included as part of the product, and adding conditions to the overall process based on external factors.

Since Android Studio is built on the IntelliJ IDEA platform it inherits most of its functionality from IntelliJ's core. It adds further Android-specific functionality to the core in the way of plug-ins. A plug-in is a software component that can be downloaded from the IntelliJ plug-in repository and installed or removed in a pluggable fashion. These plug-ins serve to enhance IntelliJ's functionality, and each one can be enabled or disabled by using the Settings window. The IntelliJ Gradle plug-in melds IntelliJ's core build system to the Gradle build system. Actions that would usually activate an application build instead invoke Gradle while the output is sent back through the IntelliJ core and formatted in a manner that is familiar to IntelliJ. This is analogous with how Android Studio's IntelliJ underpinnings have traditionally managed projects. With both Gradle and the IntelliJ environment, a simple project could contain a single module, named app, and a few other folders and files, or it could contain multiple modules with various names.

IntelliJ IDEA, on which Android Studio is founded, has been evolving for many years. Parts of this evolution are the many customization features that proliferate with each software release. These numerous customizable features, combined with hundreds of third-party plug-ins, make IntelliJ, and now by extension, Android Studio, among the most customizable and flexible Integrated Development Environments (IDEs) on the market. In fact, almost anything you can imagine being customized in an IDE is most likely customizable in Android Studio. The customizable features in Android Studio are so numerous that we cannot reasonably cover them all. Throughout this book, we have already discussed some of the most important customizable features of Android Studio, including tool buttons and default layouts, and live templates, code generation, and code styles.

Getting the most out of your app often means giving it the right visual appeal to delight your target audience. While Android makes it trivial to get up and running with one of its various template projects, sometimes you will likely need more control over the look and feel of your application. Maybe you want to change the placement of a radio button sitting next to another control, or maybe you need to create your own custom controls. We have attempted to cover the basics of designing layouts and organizing your controls so they appear correctly across the myriad of Android devices available.

Android layout designs are based on three core Android classes, Views, ViewGroups, and Activities. These are your base building blocks when it comes to painting the screen. While the user-interface packages have many more classes, most of them subclass, utilize, or are components of these core classes.

One should also take into account Android Studio's windowed environment. In order to make the best use of such limited screen space, and to keep you from being overwhelmed, Android Studio displays only a small fraction of the available windows at any given time. Some of these windows are context-sensitive and show up only when the context is appropriate, while others remain hidden until you decide to show them, or conversely remain visible until you decide to remove them.

To take full advantage of Android Studio, you need to learn the functions of these windows, as well as how and when to display them. The easiest way to manage multiple windows within Android Studio is through navigation. Android projects are typically composed of many packages, directories, and files, and an Android project of even modest complexity can contain hundreds of such assets. Your productivity with Android Studio will depend in large measure on how good you get at navigating within these assets and across them.

Android Studio is packed with many more tools geared toward Android development. And it is important to know what tools you have at your disposal. Many of these are incorporated into the various tool windows, and others are a mere keystroke away. Android Device Monitor Android Device Monitor (ADM) is a good example of one of the most powerful tools in the software development kit (SDK). It allows you to monitor your device from multiple perspectives and inspect such things as memory, CPU, network utilization, and more.

At this point, it might seem that you need to be an experienced programmer to learn Android Development. Luckily, it is not the case. If you're a beginner and wish to build a career in Android Development, then you can take up any of the online Android Development courses out there to help you gain all the knowledge to become a full-fledged Android Developer. Even if you are an experienced professional, you can still upgrade your skills from the comfort of your home.

There are many reasons why you should consider investing your time and energy into learning Android Studio tools as soon as possible.

First of all, Android is an Open Source operating system. It is a Linux based mobile operating system that makes the source code freely available for anyone to use. It also means that any changes made to the source code must be made available when a binary (a compiled and executable piece of software) is released to the public. That offers great freedom to developers by allowing them to easily adjust and modify the programming codes.

As already mentioned, Android development mainly requires knowledge of Java Programming Language. Considered as one of the easiest coding languages to learn, Java language is the first exposure to the principles of Object-Oriented design to many developers. If you have a fair knowledge of Java, then you can easily create successful Android applications. In addition, many other languages can be used for Android App Development, such as Kotlin, C++, Python, and C#. Since no language can be called the correct language for Android App Development, the choice of language remains with you only, based on objectives and preferences you set for the project.

Second of all, let's face it—Android is one of the best-selling mobile operating system worldwide. Android Developers create great mobile applications on the Android platform. As a part of their main responsibilities, they develop the apps we use on our smartphones, tablets, Android Wear, e-Readers, Google Glass, and Android TV. For all of these devices, the development fundamentals are pretty much the same as they all are powered by Android. Developers often collaborate with cross-functional teams to develop better apps with fewer bugs to ensure the responsiveness and quality of an application when it is used.

Moreover, Android apps could easily be approved and deployed in one day only. To compare, performing the same task on Apple's App Store would be ten times more challenging. In order to build an Android app, all you need to do is register yourself as a developer, create your Android application package (APK), and submit it to the Android mobile application development platform. This process is just as simple as getting yourself registered at the iOS platform.

At last, due to the growing market share of Android apps, big organizations are looking for Android Developers, which is why Android development has become the most popular professional career option nowadays.

Once you learn Android Development and start building apps, you will be able to make your Android apps reach many users worldwide. With the Android market growing rapidly, the job opportunities for Android Developers are also increasing. So if you decide to take Android Development as a career option, then you can easily get a good position in this industry.

Android professionals work under many different job designations. Your specialized expertise in mobile development can qualify you for a variety of in-demand job roles, such as Mobile Architect, Mobile Application Developer,

Android Developer, Android Engineer, and Mobile Embedded Software Engineer. Thus, whether you are a beginner or someone familiar with the Android operating system, there is no better time to improve your Android skills and start looking for new life opportunities.

Android Development is not only an easy skill to learn, but also highly in demand. By learning Android Development, you give yourself the best possible chance to reach any career goals you set. Additionally, a career in Android Development can give you all the flexibility and the ability to work from anywhere you want. Once you enter this industry, you can choose to either work from the company that you have joined or you can also choose to work from home as a freelancer. And once you get started, within no time, it is possible to land in your dream job, have that promotion, or create a successful business of your own in the field of Android Development.

Index